THE CHANGE AGENT

THE CHANGE AGENT

A Leadership Fable About Transforming
Corporate Culture

Mark Sasscer

iUniverse, Inc.
New York Lincoln Shanghai

THE CHANGE AGENT

A Leadership Fable About Transforming Corporate Culture

iUniverse books may be ordered through booksellers or by contacting:

iUniverse
2021 Pine Lake Road, Suite 100
Lincoln, NE 68512
www.iuniverse.com
1-800-Authors (1-800-288-4677)

ISBN-13: 978-0-595-38802-8 (pbk)
ISBN-13: 978-0-595-83183-8 (ebk)
ISBN-10: 0-595-38802-7 (pbk)
ISBN-10: 0-595-83183-4 (ebk)

Printed in the United States of America

To Cheryl, my wife of 20 years, for believing in me and for coaching me along the way.

To my Mom, Michael, Sean, and Ryan, for helping me "look in the mirror" and grow as a son and as a father.

Finally, to Oscar and Debbie, for 26 years of friendship and unconditional love.

CONTENTS

▼

Acknowledgments

I want to acknowledge the contributions of Maureen McNeill, who helped guide this book from lofty concept to written word; Barry Savage, who has been a wonderful business partner and who served as a dedicated advisor to this project; my delightful partner Mary Lemionet, who has been an energetic motivator in getting it done; my dear friend and gifted colleague, Susan North, Sc.D., who encouraged me to trust that I had something meaningful to say and helped me say it; my close friend Craig Linthicum, who validated that this book is congruent with who I am and what I teach; and James Landi and Gail Samis, both passionate educators and leaders, for taking the time to help refine and polish this work.

Many of the principles that inform my consulting practice and are illustrated in this book have been discussed in other books, albeit in a different context. Richard Carlson, Ph.D., author of *You Can Be Happy No Matter What*, and Aubrey Daniels, Ph.D., author of *Bringing Out the Best in People*, are two writers who have particularly inspired my work.

Also, I want to acknowledge Julie Smith, Ph.D., for introducing me to the science of behavior analysis and, also, Larry Senn, Ph.D., and Bernadette Senn for introducing me to the principles of healthy psychological functioning.

Finally, I want to thank all of the clients with whom I've had the privilege and pleasure to work. You are the real "change agents" and the ones who inspire me to do what I do—thank you!

Introduction

Corporate culture eats strategy for lunch!

When I first heard these words about 20 years ago, I had two questions: first of all, what's the definition of "corporate culture," and second, what does it mean that "culture eats strategy for lunch?" After years of experience helping leaders of large corporations and institutions change or transform their cultures, I have come to define it this way: *"corporate culture" is learned behavior resulting from organizational beliefs, biases, traditions, values, rewards, punishments, etc., in other words, all of the factors that drive the way we behave within an organizational setting.*

When I thought about the answer to my second question—what does it mean to say that "corporate culture eats strategy for lunch"—I reflected on the impact that human behavior has on the execution of business strategies and initiatives. While working in the leadership ranks of the telecommunications industry for 15 years and later consulting with senior executives of Fortune 500 companies, I have seen many well-crafted strategies and worthwhile initiatives fail, struck down by negative corporate cultures. These failures come at great cost to the corporations involved.

The good news is that, with commitment and courage, corporate culture can be changed or transformed—and, with awareness, focus, and clear communication, virtually anyone in a leadership role can be a *change agent.* Culture is shaped in large measure by its leaders, by how the leaders, themselves, behave. This is vital to the discussion of how corporate culture is created because *employees mirror the behaviors of their leaders. Corporate culture starts at the top and cascades throughout the ranks.* The *change agent*, through his or her behavior and leadership, can motivate and inspire that process.

When you look at the behaviors that leaders model and the behaviors they reward and punish, informally and formally [i.e., through corporate Human Resource (HR) Systems], you can almost predict how effectively their strategies and initiatives will be executed. No matter how good their corporate direction is, it takes people to get behind that direction and implement it. If people are working in an environment where they don't feel motivated to offer their best, execution will suffer.

According to research conducted by the Gallup Organization in early 2001, fewer than 30% of American workers are fully engaged at work. The cost of a disengaged workforce runs into millions of dollars annually. My own experience supports the Gallup findings; most senior executives tell me that less than half of their employees give *discretionary effort. Discretionary effort is the effort employers get when employees move from compliance to commitment,* when they willingly volunteer behavior over and above the minimum necessary to do their jobs. It is corporate culture that motivates or suppresses *discretionary effort.* Further, it is organizational leaders who have the greatest influence on shaping corporate culture.

Based on experience, I believe that mastering the art of culture change or transformation continues to be a challenge for many leaders—in part, because assessing their corporate culture objectively, understanding its impact on execution and results, and then taking concrete steps to change or transform the culture requires courage—the courage to embark on a journey of self awareness and reflection, a journey of personal transformation within the context of organizational transformation—*the courage to be a change agent.*

This book, a leadership fable, is not only for executives of large companies, though. If you supervise a team, manage a business unit or functional unit, own a small business or simply want to learn more about the impact that leadership behavior has on organizational performance, this book is for you. It will help you to become a *change agent.*

As you read this book, you will be introduced to a fictitious company, Horton & Oliver, and to its senior leaders. You will probably soon discover that you have seen, in action, the characteristics of this company or its leaders before—perhaps in your own organization. Please note, however, that all of the people and companies described in this story have been created for purposes of illustration only. This is a fable.

As you enjoy the story of culture change at Horton & Oliver, think of your own potential as a *change agent.* And remember this—as you read and learn more about what is behind the quote, "culture eats strategy for lunch," ask yourself what percentage of the people around you (i.e., your direct reports, peers, and other colleagues) volunteer discretionary effort each and every day. Then look in the mirror and ask yourself, "What more can I do to improve this?"

To assist you on your journey as a *change agent*, at the end of each chapter, you will find a series of questions designed to challenge you to think about how you could be even more effective at influencing change within your own company or organization. Spend some time considering each of the questions and giving each one your most honest response.

If you want to be an agent of change to increase the number of people in your organization who give discretionary effort routinely, and to realize the powerful benefits of doing so, this book will help. Enjoy!

Mark Sasscer

The Horton & Oliver (H&O) Leadership Team

Michael: The Chief Executive Officer (CEO) is 63 years old and has worked at Horton & Oliver for 29 years, seven as its CEO. He has an M.B.A. and a B.A. in history.

Edward: The Chairman of the Board is 67 years old. He has served on the H&O Board for 10 years, two as Chairman.

Jennifer (Jen): The new Chief Operating Officer (COO) is 50 years old. She has an M.B.A. and a B.S. in psychology.

David: The Chief Counsel for H&O is 58 years old. He joined Horton & Oliver eight years ago. He has a J.D. and a B.S. in business administration.

Alan: The Executive Vice President (EVP) of Human Resources (HR) is 52 years old and has worked 24 years with Horton & Oliver. He has a B.A. in English literature, a B.S. in business administration and an M.S. in organization development.

Kim: The Chief Financial Officer (CFO) is 39 years old and has worked for 14 years at Horton & Oliver. She has a B.S. in accounting, an M.B.A. and is a CPA.

Roger: The Executive Vice President (EVP) of Sales is 45 years old. He has worked for seven years at Horton & Oliver and has a B.S. in business administration.

PROLOGUE

───────────── ▼ ─────────────

"I can't think when I've been to a less happy Happy Hour," Roger said. "You people are way too gloomy for me."

"Let's see, Roger," Kim snarled. "Operating costs are up, we're losing market share to companies who benefited from hiring those we laid off and this afternoon Michael had to present the Board with our worst numbers ever. Are you the only one who doesn't think we all have nooses for neckties and scarves? In a nutshell, our days are numbered."

"Speaking of Michael," Alan cut in, "I know he's had a terrible day, but I thought he was planning to join us."

No one answered Alan. No one was in much of a mood to talk. Kim's little speech was all too familiar to them. When Michael did arrive, they greeted their captain with all the enthusiasm of crew members on a sinking ship.

"How did it go this afternoon?" David asked.

Michael paused and took a deep breath before answering. "It was pretty bad."

"Basically, I've been given one last chance. Obviously, the Board was unhappy with our results—make no mistake about that. I reminded them that we've hired a new COO. Jennifer starts Monday and the search firm says she's a specialist at turning companies like ours around—something she called 'culture change.' The Board wants to see improved results—immediately!"

"You all know Edward, our Chairman," Michael continued. "You'll be seeing more of him. He's going to personally evaluate our progress. He'll be stopping in occasionally—unannounced. I'm to forward our business results to him on a biweekly basis. Believe me, Edward will be watching us closely and looking for early signs of improvement."

"Frankly, this is better news than I was expecting. Each one of us has been given another chance. Let's make it count!"

PART I

▼

The Journey Begins

CHAPTER 1

▼

DEFINING THE CASE FOR CHANGE

"The harder the conflict, the more glorious the triumph."
—Thomas Paine

Michael knows this could be the end of his career. After nearly 30 years, it is time to consider his legacy. Now he realizes that his legacy depends, in part, on Jennifer (Jen), a woman he barely knows. He needs her, as his new COO, to bring fresh eyes to Horton & Oliver and to help find solutions to the company's problems.

When he took over as CEO, Horton & Oliver was already beginning to drift away from its glory days. Today, those days are a distant memory. Despite this, in his seven years at the helm, he knows he's become a popular leader. People like him. They respect him. They understand that H&O is his life's work. The people who work for the company trust Michael, and he feels the weight of that trust. However, at this point in time, the Board is less concerned about Michael's relationship with H&O's employees—the Board is more concerned about improving results.

And the Board has plenty to be concerned about. The financials are just one indicator—and they spell trouble. It has been four years since H&O has launched a highly successful new product line. During this period, production costs have risen significantly. When that situation forced prices up, customers complained. Before long, more complaints were pouring in—new ones: service is slow or unresponsive and the quality of Horton & Oliver's products is slipping.

While operating expenses continue to climb, Horton & Oliver's share of the market is shrinking.

The first signs of real trouble came in Michael's fourth year at the helm. When the economy took a dive, it took H&O down with it. Although his EVP of Sales, Roger, continued to cite economic conditions to explain poor sales, Michael— and the Board—knew that, by now, Horton & Oliver should have executed a new strategy in response to outside forces. That's what successful companies do.

Last year, when the Chairman of the Board recommended a consultant, some- one Edward said he knew to be highly skilled at cutting costs, Michael argued that this approach was simply a "quick fix" and would not address the root causes of H&O's problems. Edward refused to listen and, in the end, Michael reluc- tantly agreed.

Edward demanded immediate results and the consultant got them: costs were slashed in a dramatic series of layoffs. Some senior, but mostly middle- and lower-level employees were cut. In the downsizing, Michael's greatest fear had come true: this temporary fix had taken a serious toll on morale. When he walked through the headquarters building last week, he not only saw the effects of the layoffs, but he also heard them. He overheard one assistant complaining, and then heard another saying she was happy to have a job—for as long as it would last. But, if she could find something better, she was going to go for it.

The recent departure of Richard, his COO, was the toughest for Michael to swallow. While Richard wasn't what anyone would consider a dynamic leader— the consultant pointed that out early on—Richard had been the first to speak up about Horton & Oliver's problems. He warned that the company's cost structure and its prices were out of line with the marketplace and complained that the sales staff resisted change. He even suggested they were too comfortable with estab- lished product lines to sell something new. More than one person has worried aloud that Richard was a scapegoat. In his heart, Michael feared they were right.

The new COO, Jen, starts work on Monday, and Michael hopes she is as tal- ented as her reputation suggests. She'll need to be. She has developed a solid rep- utation as a change agent who can turn struggling companies around. Her reputation suggests that Jen creates work environments in which things hap- pen—people are inspired to do their best and produce results. H&O needs a turn-around, and Michael hopes Jen will help make it happen.

When they met at industry conferences, Michael was impressed by Jen's confi- dent and upbeat demeanor. When Jen interviewed at Horton & Oliver, Michael seized the opportunity to ask her about her successes at her last two companies. Both times, she joined failing companies and deftly managed to be an agent of change: growing revenues while reducing costs and improving customer service, productivity, and morale. In interviews, she had talked about "culture change," making a statement Michael found compelling. She told him and others that *it doesn't matter how good your vision and strategy are if your corporate culture is broken. "Culture,"* she said, *"eats strategy for lunch!"*

Michael has been wondering whether the culture at H&O is at the heart of its problems. Over the past two years, every attempt he has made to implement a new strategy or initiative has failed. Whenever the executive team discussed this issue, there always seemed to be someone or something, other than themselves, to blame for poor execution. It has gotten even worse during the past year because of the layoffs. The old H&O "can-do" spirit seems to be gone.

On top of everything else, their top customer, Fargo, Inc., is threatening to leave. A long-time friend of Michael's, the CEO there was the first customer to point out what Michael now realizes is fact: Horton & Oliver's prices have risen, but service and quality have declined and are nowhere near their once-high standards. What was most disturbing for Michael to hear was that H&O's customer service representatives often complain to customers about the state of affairs at Horton & Oliver. Michael shared these concerns with his executive team. The consensus was that this was an inevitable consequence of the downsizing "Edward's consultant" initiated.

Obviously, the new COO will have to hit the ground running. Jen was an early favorite in the accelerated search process. Even as an executive search firm was being secured, Michael and a Board member suggested hiring her based on her track record for building high-performing organizations. There were other candidates, but Jen quickly emerged as the best choice.

Michael doesn't envy her. His first days at Horton & Oliver had been marked with exciting new challenges. Jen's first days would hold challenges, all right, but much more of the uphill type than he had experienced. For example, the executive team has committed to the Board that, this year, they will drive an additional $50 million in cost out of the business through process-improvement efforts, while improving quality and customer service levels. In order to accomplish this, they will need the help of every H&O employee. Michael realizes they will need to regain their "can-do" spirit. That is the immediate challenge Jen faces.

Your Turn: Be a *Change Agent*

1. How would you describe the culture of your company or organization? What are the patterns of behavior, productive and unproductive, that employees there exhibit day in and day out?

2. Which of these patterns do you see in your own behavior? Which of these patterns would your colleagues say they see in your behavior?

3. Overall, how does the culture of your company or organization impact the execution of business strategies and initiatives?

4. What is the impact of your company's or organization's culture on customer service, employee satisfaction, productivity, and financial performance?

5. What percentage of people in your company or organization volunteer discretionary effort every day? How much discretionary effort do you volunteer each day?

Corporate culture eats strategy for lunch.

CHAPTER 2

▼

INTRODUCING THE
CHANGE AGENT

"People seldom improve when they have no other model but themselves to copy."
—Oliver Goldsmith

Michael isn't the only one spending Sunday evening thinking of what Monday morning will bring. Over dinner, Jen and her husband, Ted, talk about the challenges that she'll face. Jen is generally excited about her new position and confident in her abilities. This new company, however, is twice the size of any with which she has worked. When she was interviewing for the position, more than one Board member suggested that the CEO was getting ready to retire and that they like to fill key positions from within the company. Could she see herself as CEO in a couple of years? It isn't the first time such a question has come up, yet Jen is unwilling to entertain such thinking at this point in time.

While they're enjoying another glass of wine, Jen and Ted talk over what she knows thus far about her new employer. She has met the CEO several times at industry meetings and likes him. After she accepted the position, she and Michael talked about his goals for the executive team. He has let her know that he holds the CFO, Kim, in high regard and is confident that Jen and Kim will become good partners in turning things around. Jen remembers meeting Kim during the interview process and recognizes in Kim many of the habits she used to indulge in herself. It seems to Jen that Kim has concluded that the only way to break through the glass ceiling is by becoming a workaholic and by making sure everyone is aware of the hours she puts in on the company's behalf. In striving for what she thought of as perfection, Jen remembers working long hours herself and, in the process, being hard on others, unwilling to accept normal human frailties. Jen stops herself, realizing that her first impression of someone she barely knows has turned to judgment. One valuable lesson she learned early on in her career was to **become aware of destructive thoughts. Choosing to criticize Kim—even in her own mind—was unfair to both of them. Jen knows that negative thoughts lead to negative behaviors.**

Before long, Jen and Ted get to an important issue: with this much responsibility, Jen is worried about continuing to maintain a healthy balance between her personal life and her professional one. Ted's job is every bit as demanding, but, so far, they have been able to reserve most of their weekends for personal time. With both of their children leading nearly independent lives—Anna is twenty and in her third year of college; Tony, who's twenty-five, has a good job and his own place—she and Ted have many of their weekends to themselves. Less of their time is spent parenting. This may be the ideal time to take on more challenges at work. Together, they can ensure that they make time for one another on weekends.

As she falls asleep, Jen's thoughts are whirling: she remembers her conversations with the CEO, her impressions of the executive team and many other details. Finally, she turns to the guidance of her former coach. Jen thinks about how fortunate she was to have joined her first executive team when Brian was brought in as a consultant. Having taught at a prestigious business school for much of his career, Brian now works to strengthen corporate teams and organizations. Not only has she learned his lessons well, but she also has had two opportunities now to watch him in action as he showed business leaders the path toward building a high-performing team and organization. In many cases, Brian stays on to coach individual team members. He was Jen's coach just five years ago. Brian shared lessons with Jen that she has proven in her own experience time and again. **The lesson that she needs to live now is: Meet people where they are. Jen decides she'll approach her new colleagues and surroundings with curiosity and set aside judgment.**

Week One, Monday

As she wakes up Monday morning, she can still hear Brian's voice: "Meet people where they are." **Go in and observe: watch, listen (there will be plenty of time for talk later).** Jen holds on to Brian's words as she recalls another voice. Her new CEO, Michael, has said there is an immediate, demanding need for strong leadership. Jen arrives at Horton & Oliver, parks her car, takes a deep breath, and is ready to begin her new job.

Jen walks through the doors and looks around at the lobby, taking it all in from a fresh perspective. The Horton & Oliver building is gracious, the lobby is large, the walls are hung with modern art, and there are beautiful, fresh-cut flowers on the reception desk. While the art is modern, everything else about Horton & Oliver seems conservative. Jen notices a few employees milling about, but none of them seems to be in a hurry to get to work. She steps onto the elevator and pushes the button for the top floor. The special key that she received in the same FedEx package with her parking pass gives her access to the executive suite.

Here, the furnishings are even finer than those in the lobby. Another bouquet—larger than the first—graces a mahogany table in the vestibule. She takes a minute to smell the flowers before finding her office. It's 7:30 a.m. on a Monday morning; she wonders what it costs to get fresh flowers delivered on that schedule. Her office is spacious and well appointed. As she sets some family pictures on the credenza, Jen looks out the window. Below her office, the executive parking lot has just four cars in it—there are eight spots reserved. The larger employee lot is equally bare, only one-third full.

Jen hears a tap on her door and turns to meet her new executive assistant. In their brief conversation, Jen learns that Rose has been with the company for thirty-four years—even longer than Michael. As sorry as she was to see Richard leave, Rose says, she didn't think seriously of retiring. After all, what would she do with herself? Jen is on the verge of asking more about her new assistant when Rose hands her a page of appointments for the day and apologetically lets her know that her first meeting begins in ten minutes. In fact, the day is completely booked with conference calls and meetings. Before rushing off to her first executive team meeting, Jen asks Rose to schedule a lunch for the two of them. "Let's get out of the office and take a little time to talk and get to know one another. And let's not cut ourselves short: I'd like you to book ninety minutes."

It's 7:55 a.m. when Jen arrives at the Boardroom. She remembers the man who opens the door and enters with her as David, Chief Council to Horton & Oliver. David is tall, well dressed and seems very serious. Jen guesses that he is in his late fifties. As they make their way across the room, Jen isn't sure which is more surprising, the fresh fruit, freshly baked pastries and croissants, and gourmet coffees on the antique sideboard or the fact that she and David are the only two who have arrived before 8:00 a.m. Having held the door for her, David now pours Jen a cup of coffee and offers her cream and sugar. She sets down her elegant china cup and saucer to accept the silver sugar bowl from him. Jen stirs in a sugar cube with a silver spoon and begins to make small talk. David is single, but when Jen fills him in on her family, he pulls out photos of nieces and nephews and shows a level of interest in children that Jen usually hears only from devoted parents.

Michael and another man join them at about two minutes after 8:00 a.m. Jen recognizes Alan, the EVP of Human Resources (HR), from the search process. Alan is an African-American man, about fifty-two. Like David, he is well dressed and somewhat soft-spoken. When Michael heads for the sideboard, Alan and David fall into an animated conversation. Jen overhears them talking about a series of diversity workshops Alan would like to initiate. He's doubtful that there will be room in this year's budget. David's comments are supportive, but they are not optimistic. Jen finds herself liking these new colleagues. They are open with each other and respectful.

As the group turns to small talk, Jen has a chance to take in the rest of the Boardroom. Portraits of past chief executives and Board chairmen line the paneled walls. The large mahogany conference table is stunning and obviously an antique. The color scheme in the room combines hunter greens, rich burgundies, and creams, and reminds Jen of the rooms in men's clubs in old movies. All that's missing is the cigar smoke.

The four of them are still standing and chatting when Roger, EVP of Sales, arrives. He is a bit younger than the others and very talkative; he's been reporting to Michael on an interim basis since Richard, the former COO, left the company. Once he has his coffee, Roger makes his way to Michael and begins regaling him with stories about his weekend golf game.

Jen looks at her watch. Wasn't this meeting scheduled for 8:00 a.m.? She's due to meet with her direct reports in Operations at 9:00 a.m.

When, at 8:15 a.m., Michael suggests they begin, Jen finds a place at the table and goes into her pre-meeting routine: cell phone off, journal out, and pen ready. Jen's leather-bound journal is the latest in a long series that began with a gift from Brian. She has developed a habit of note taking that includes not only her "to-do" list, but also her observations, questions, and ideas. If there is an issue to be resolved, Jen commits it to her journal. When an answer emerges, that goes into the journal, too. With her tools close at hand, Jen scans the table, then the room for an agenda. There is none.

It takes several minutes for the others to take their seats and for the meeting to begin. Just as Michael begins the meeting (it's 8:20 a.m. already), Kim flies into the room. While she seems rushed at first, the CFO takes time to pour herself a cup of coffee and dish some fruit onto a plate. Before Michael can begin speaking again, Kim announces: "I had a great phone conversation with the Director of our manufacturing division last night. We've been looking for ways to streamline production. I think we've really got something. Michael, I'll fill you in later."

Michael nods, then picks up where he left off, extending a warm welcome to Jen. "I must say I've been impressed with Jennifer since we met at a convention in Tucson four years ago," he tells the executive team. Michael reviews Jen's resumé for the group and is singing her praises when Roger's cell phone rings. No one but Jen seems surprised when Roger takes the call, waving to Michael to continue. Michael tells the group that he is expecting them to partner with Jen and that, together, they can restore Horton & Oliver to the company it once was. He adds that he is confident Jen will bring a fresh, new perspective to H&O that is long overdue. Returning to his earlier theme, Michael reminds the group of his hopes that the executive team will form lasting partnerships for the benefit of the company. He looks at Kim, who smiles and nods in reply.

Jen is struck by the thought that she has seen this kind of meeting before. She realizes there is no sense of urgency among those at the table. She steals a glance at her watch as Michael begins discussing the state of the company. It's 8:40! Jen is wondering just how long it will take to get from the Boardroom to her next meeting.

Michael finishes his thirty-five-minute oration and suggests that they go around the table, giving those in the room a chance to introduce themselves to "Jennifer." As politely as she can, she asks them to please call her Jen. She quickly points out that her next meeting, her first with her direct reports on the Operations team, is in less than ten minutes. She apologizes and says that her schedule reflects that the executive team meeting was supposed to run from 8:00 a.m. until 9:00 a.m. Kim chuckles quietly. "Don't worry, your schedule is correct," she tells Jen. "But they'll wait for you. They're used to it." Roger's laugh is a little louder. "Take it from me, Jennifer," he says, "sooner or later you'll find out that the only people who really produce around here work on this floor."

David's tone is more studied and professional.

"Jennifer," he begins.

"Please, I prefer Jen."

"Jen, you'll have to excuse some of my colleagues. They have a tendency to downplay the efforts of others in the company."

Looks of surprise flash across Kim's and Roger's faces. They are quickly replaced with frowns. Michael nervously clears his throat. "Well, I'm sure you'll have a chance to get to know everyone a bit before our Wednesday meeting." He quickly draws the meeting to a close.

Jen heads out wondering whether she's made a mistake asking Michael to cut the meeting short. He is, after all, the CEO. She also takes a minute to think about Kim's remarks. If Jen's new team is accustomed to their leader arriving late, she will likely have to do more to earn their trust. ***She knows she must demonstrate in her own behavior the qualities she hopes to see in her team.***

As she goes from meeting to meeting over the course of her first week, the notes in her journal confirm the pattern she is seeing. Every meeting has the tone of that first one: agendas are either absent or poorly constructed, meetings start late, people straggle in after that and get up to leave before it's over, cell phones ring and are answered, and, when the meetings do end, there is no real closure—no agreed-upon decisions, no next steps planned. She wonders how that can be in this day and age.

It is mid-day Wednesday when she finally has a chance to ask Rose how her calendar became so full of meetings even before she'd arrived to plan them. Rose seems surprised by the question. "Those were the meetings Richard scheduled every week," she says. "I was sure you'd want them too, since they'd worked for him for so long." Jen couldn't help but wonder whether they had.

She answers Rose, "It's fine for this week, but please don't schedule anything for next week unless it's with the CEO, someone from the executive team, or someone who reports directly to me. I see you've scheduled lunch for next Monday. That will give us a chance to talk about our work styles and chat about the meeting schedule."

The week brings three meetings with the executive team and Jen sees the same patterns in these meetings that she has seen company-wide. There are poor agendas to begin with and no closure at the finish. At each gathering, she finds herself distracted by the many side conversations going on. There seems to be plenty of agreement around the table, but that agreement is gone once the team has left the room. When the executive team does engage in a discussion at a meeting Friday morning, Kim and Roger tend to dominate the proceedings, sweeping aside the contributions and suggestions of Alan and David.

On Friday afternoon at 5:00 p.m., Jen is introduced to another Horton & Oliver tradition when the executive team gathers in Michael's office. A bar comes out from the wall and Michael offers them each a drink. Jen learns that any member of the executive team or the Board has a standing invitation to Friday Happy Hour. Shrimp cocktail, imported cheeses and meats, crackers and breads, and other snacks are spread on the table. Twenty-five-year-old scotch stands alongside imported vodka. Today, it's just the executive team. Except for Alan, who has a glass of iced tea, each one mixes a drink. Jen silently chides herself for noting that this is the first time all week that the team has met on time with a common agenda!

After everyone has had time to fix a plate, Michael pops the cork on a bottle of Dom Perignon and congratulates Jen on her first week with the company. Jen thanks him. Afterward, Michael and Jen are chatting, comparing plans for the weekend, when David and Alan approach them. David says, "Alan and I were just talking, Jen, and we were wondering what your impressions are after your first week, or is it too early to ask?" Jen takes a minute to consider what Brian would advise her to do. This is a moment of truth, but is it a moment for truth? Would she be better off dodging this question? She remembers another of Brian's lessons: Authenticity. ***"Be authentic at all times."***

Jen takes a deep breath and takes the opportunity to speak openly. "Well, since you've asked, I have a few observations. When I sit in on meetings, everyone nods as if s/he agrees, but I wonder whether there is real agreement. Let me give you an example. When I sat down with a Production team Wednesday, everyone got along very well and seemed to leave the table aligned. But when I stopped to use the ladies room after the meeting, I happened to overhear two of the women I'd just met airing their real concerns and they didn't agree at all with what was said in the meeting. I worry that we are sacrificing real discussion because people are afraid to disagree. Obviously, this hurts execution. You guys have been to as many meetings this week as I have. What patterns of behavior do you see?"

Kim and Roger have joined the conversation and for several minutes the group indulges in criticizing their employees. "You're absolutely right! These people act like they're afraid to speak up." "And when they do offer something worthwhile, getting others to agree and buy in seems impossible." "It's amazing to me these people don't recognize good ideas when they see them set on the table!" "Well, of course not! They're too busy protecting their own turf to agree with anyone else."

Jen listens as the group takes hold of this subject. When she asks, "Why do you think that is?" the responses follow familiar themes. "You just can't find quality people who want to work anymore." "It's the new generation of workers in this country—they want everything handed to them." "We lost a lot of people in last year's layoffs—now I wonder if we kept the wrong ones!" "The people we have now are lazy. They completely lack focus."

Jen has one more question. "I've been to three meetings of our team. What do you think I've observed?" Kim is quick to answer, "A team of people working hard to turn this ship around!" David, however, looks as though he's just seen a ghost as he says quietly, "The employees act just the way we do." Alan, mustering up some courage, says, "I'm embarrassed to say it, but you're right, David."

"Thanks a lot, guys," Kim says sharply. "You're saying we're the problem around here?"

"I don't know," Alan answers her. Kim and Roger turn to pour themselves another drink and are soon involved in their own conversation.

"What I've learned from past experience," Jen says, "is that, if I hope to influence someone else's behavior, I have to change my own behavior first."

After a pause, Michael turns to Jen, "So you're saying we have to change?" Jen is ready: "We do, Michael. ***Employees mirror the behaviors of their leaders. If we want people to act differently, we have to define the behaviors we want and model them ourselves.***"

Michael says, "I want to hear more about this at our staff meeting Monday morning. I want to hear what you did at your last company."

At the sound of Michael's question, Kim has returned to the conversation. She abruptly tells Jen she'll call her over the weekend to prep for Monday's meeting. "What's your cell phone number?" Kim asks.

Jen is polite, but ready with her answer: "My personal policy is that, barring emergencies, weekends are personal time. Is there any chance we can talk early Monday morning?"

"Sure. Whatever," Kim shoots back. Then, a little too loudly to be directed at Roger alone, Kim says, "I'd heard there were women who had it all. I never thought I'd actually meet one!"

Jen is up early Saturday, reviewing her journal and making some notes for Monday's executive team meeting. Over the years, Jen and Ted have made a point of finding a balance between work and home. When the children came along, and as each has taken on more responsibility at work, Jen and Ted have helped each other adjust. They are confident Jen's new job won't pose a problem.

Jen's daughter, Anna, is home this weekend and they plan to spend the day together. When Anna comes in carrying a mug of coffee, Jen looks at the clock. She has done a lot of business planning in ninety minutes. Jen asks her daughter if she'd like some pancakes.

Breakfast is very relaxed. Anna is full of stories from college and her lively storytelling has Ted and Jen fully entertained. Over coffee, Ted and Anna turn to Jen. They are anxious to hear about her first week at Horton & Oliver.

Jen describes the facilities and personalities in positive terms. After a brief pause she adds, "It's pretty clear that some members of this team regularly have business conversations during the weekends. I've already picked up some resistance to keeping my boundaries in place."

"Resistance from Michael?" Ted asks.

"No. Not yet, anyway."

"You know, I honestly don't know how workaholics do it," says Ted, his exasperation showing. "I seriously need my weekends. The time I spend with you guys is important to me—especially when tensions at work kick in. It's on the weekend that I get a chance to re-charge my batteries. This change of focus makes me a better performer at work."

"Believe me, Ted. I agree with you." Jen says quickly. "I don't really think it's a question of there being too much work to take care of in five days—even considering the layoffs. In fact, this is where I think I can make a real difference at H&O. There are so many ways we can improve efficiency at the office. When we take care of that, I really don't think there will be a need to sacrifice weekends to get the job done. I think I can help this team see that we have plenty of time Monday through Friday. We just need to make better use of it."

Week Two, Monday

On Monday morning, after meeting with Kim for thirty minutes, Jen approaches Michael in his office at 7:30 a.m. She's curious to know whether he had any more reflections over the weekend about what they had talked about Friday afternoon. Just as important, Jen wants to make sure she clearly understands what he wants her to talk about at the 8:00 a.m. meeting. Michael shares that he found the Friday discussion to be interesting, albeit unsettling.

"Everything you said—as hard as it was to hear—rang true with me," Michael tells Jen. "It makes sense that people throughout the company would act the way we do. And I know that's not the way we want them to act. It's so obvious! I'm embarrassed to say I didn't see this before."

"You know Michael, this is one of the reasons I took this job," she answers. "Don't look so surprised. I sincerely love challenges like this one because I've seen what can be accomplished *immediately* and over the long haul. There are changes we can make right now that will let everyone know that this is a new day and that things will be different."

"Like what?"

This is an important moment for Jen—but an even more important moment for Michael. For Jen to show Michael that she has the answers will serve Jen well. However, if Michael is allowed to realize that he already has the answers and only needs the right questions to bring them out, it will serve Michael, Jen, and everyone at Horton & Oliver far better. Jen sees that **her role is to help Michael and the team discover the wisdom that is within them.**

"Well," Jen answers, "let's look at two areas: meeting management and cost cutting. What changes would you make at the executive level that could have an impact on our own effectiveness and on how staff members perceive us?"

"There are some things that seem obvious to me now," Michael answers. "At our meetings, there are rules we should agree to: no cell phones, for one thing. I hate it when they go off. We should have better agendas. In fact, the agenda should go out seventy-two hours before the meeting so everyone has time to prepare. Lately, it seems as though no one reads the materials I send out in advance. This has to change."

"That would be a great start," says Jen. "In the spirit of having open and honest communication, we could adopt a rule that **we have the real conversations in the meeting room. What we say, we say together and not behind one another's backs. Then, we must speak with one voice when we leave the room.** While we're talking about meetings, Michael, I also think we need to work on 'focus.' Our biggest issues right now—service, costs and quality—are all about how we take care of our customers. What can we do to bring the focus back to our customers?"

"Amen!" Michael answers passionately. "If we can't link what we do to the customer, why are we doing it? That's a sure way to put ourselves out of business. We shouldn't even be meeting if it isn't to benefit our customers."

"I agree completely," says Jen.

"We're talking about that clear agenda again," Michael adds. "Each and every meeting has to have an agenda that is obviously focused on our customers, directly or indirectly. That goes for our team and for the rest of the company. This is basic business, but I feel like we've lost track of the basics."

"But what you're talking about will send a strong, positive message," Jen agrees. "Let's talk for a minute about costs—reducing costs. What can we do immediately to convey a message that we're serious about continuing to cut costs, without any more downsizing—that additional expense reductions are vital to our survival?"

"Oh, please, Jen. Don't tell me you want to do away with our executive assistants or our company cars. I'm not sure making minor changes like that will get us out of the situation we're in."

"What I'm thinking of is more basic than that, Michael. It's about how we act. **Those of us on the executive team need to behave as though we own this company, as though every dollar we spend is a dollar of our own money. In my**

former company, we called this accountability. We continually asked our-
selves: 'What more can I do to influence the outcomes we want to see as a
company?' I can tell you right now, if I owned this company, you can be sure
that we'd have our lunch in the company lunch room, not the executive dining
room. We'd have our ears to the ground and know what was happening in the
company. And I have to wonder, can we really afford fresh flowers every morning?"

This time, Michael is less enthusiastic. "You're new here, Jen. Eating lunch
together in the executive dining room has become a tradition here. It's one of the
few times we have to really connect with one another on an informal basis. But I
have to admit, I see your point. You know, Jen, making changes like this around
here isn't going to be easy. We're—and I include myself in this—pretty stuck in
our old ways. Over the past two years, I've gotten very frustrated at our inability
to execute new initiatives."

"I understand what you mean, Michael, but I think there is an opportunity
here," Jen tells him. *"Early successes are important motivators in any change*
process. I think the combination of closing the executive dining room to save
money and eating lunch in the cafeteria to reconnect with employees will send
powerful signals to the rest of the company that we are sincere in our efforts to
change the culture at Horton & Oliver."

"Michael, there is only one person you can truly change, and that's you. If
we're going to expect this company to change, we're going to have to lead the
way, with each of us choosing to change the way we think and behave. It won't
be easy, but it must begin with us. *Culture change begins at the top!"*

Michael looks at the clock; it's ten minutes before 8:00 a.m. "Well, if change
begins with me, I'd better get going so I can be on time for our eight o'clock
meeting."

"Michael, I think you're on the right track," Jen assures him. "At the end of
the day, it will be your leadership and your example that make us successful. Let's
walk together; I have one last question for you. What could I share at 8:00 a.m.
that you believe would add the most value in terms of where we need to go?"

"I want to understand more about what you mean when you talk about corporate culture change. I'd like to hear about the work that you did at your previous
company."

Your Turn: Be a *Change Agent*

1. In meetings and one-on-one with colleagues, how often are you authentic; i.e., how often do you say what you really think and feel? What is the impact of this choice, sharing or not sharing what you think and feel, on relationships and results?

2. What percentage of the time do you approach new ideas, people, and situations with an attitude of curiosity versus judgment? What is the impact on your relationships and results when you use an attitude of curiosity? What is the impact when you use an attitude of judgment?

3. What productive and unproductive behaviors do you observe in your team that "mirror" your own behaviors?

4. How consistently do you hold yourself accountable for your company's or organization's performance? What more can you do to behave as though you own the company or organization?

5. How willing are you to change your own behavior?

Employees mirror the behaviors of their leaders.

CHAPTER 3

▼

TAKING THE FIRST STEPS

"A journey of a thousand miles must begin with a single step."
—Chinese proverb

Until Friday afternoon, life at Horton & Oliver seemed to Alan like something out of the *Twilight Zone*. The pressure to turn things around is definitely on, yet no one on the executive team has introduced any solutions lately—it's as though the team is in a state of paralysis. Then Jen dropped the bomb on them, tactfully, but honestly, pointing out the lack of focus and commitment that he had been troubled by himself. Alan is ready to finally see some change at Horton & Oliver. Jen hasn't told them anything he didn't already know, but he's never tried to point any of it out to the rest of the team himself. He begins to wonder why.

Alan and David are already in the room having their coffee when Michael and Jen arrive at the Monday meeting at about three minutes to 8:00 a.m. Before taking their seats, they pour themselves some coffee. By 8:00 a.m., both Kim and Roger are still missing. Michael begins the meeting on time without them. After allowing a few minutes for small talk, Michael outlines his agenda for the meeting. It's about 8:07 a.m. when Kim and Roger come breezing in. Roger's cell phone is to his ear and he is speaking loudly. They are startled to see that others are seated and that the meeting has obviously started. Roger says, in a quiet voice, "Listen, babe, I'll have to call you back." Michael greets each of the late arrivals, but Jen notices that neither is apologetic for being tardy.

Michael picks up where he left off. "Let me tell you how I'd like to spend our hour together this morning. First, I have a few observations, and then I'll turn things over to Jen so she can talk to us about corporate culture.

"I found our conversation Friday afternoon to be very enlightening," Michael continues. "I spent time over the weekend giving both our company and our team a lot of thought. One thing that made sense to me on Friday was when Jen said that employees mirror the behaviors of their leaders. I'm clear that I have not been a very good role model over the past few years."

"Michael, don't you think you're being a little bit hard on yourself?" Kim cuts in.

Michael's tone is stern as he answers her. "No, Kim. The problem is I haven't been hard enough. So, if we're going to change this company, I'm going to have to change the way I do things, and I'm going to ask you to join me by considering the example you set. Before I turn the agenda over to Jen to hear about what she did at her previous company, I'd like to establish some new ground rules for this team and for our meetings. My expectation is that you will model these ground rules for your own teams, too."

Michael walks over to a flip chart and writes as he says:

- Start on time and end on time

- Have a detailed agenda

Michael stops for a moment and looks to the team. A few are hunting for something to write on, but all are paying attention. He opens up the discussion and asks for the team's ideas: "What else should we have on this list?"

Alan speaks up: "Turn off cell phones."

At that moment, Roger's cell phone rings. Everyone laughs. Roger glances at his phone for the caller's number and then turns it off. "Sorry," he says sheepishly.

"Thank you, Roger. Any other rules we should have?"

"It's not enough to have an agenda. We need to be clear about which items are for discussion and which ones require a decision. In fact, we need to get the agenda in time to read it and prepare for the meeting," David offers.

"And we have to really listen to and understand what each of us is saying," Alan adds.

As the discussion continues and more items are suggested, Jen is quiet, but she offers nonverbal support. Michael adds these additional suggestions from the team to the list on the chart:

- Turn cell phones off

- Distribute agenda before meetings—identify discussion and decision items

- Read agenda and prepare for meetings in advance

- Listen for understanding

- Conclude meetings by reviewing action items and responsibilities

- Focus on how the discussion relates to the customer

Then he turns to the group. "Good job, I really like this list of ground rules! I think the last one on our list is especially important. If we go to a meeting and there is no direct or indirect link to the customer, we have to question why we're having the meeting."

"I have one more rule to add and it may be the most important," Michael tells them. *"I want to hear what you're really thinking.* What you really want to say, I want said in this room. I don't want to have the 'real conversations' taking place in hallways or private offices. *If we're going to turn this ship around, we have to be brutally honest when discussing issues. Also, after having these discussions, we have to be united and speak with one voice when addressing the organization."*

Michael returns to the flipchart and adds:

- Have open and honest communication

- Speak with one voice

"Now," Michael continues, "I want to hear what you think about all of this." Except for Kim and Roger, each team member nods in agreement.

Roger is quick to recover. "I have to say, Michael, even knowing that our team is keeping the customer in mind will make my Sales guys feel better and help them dig in."

Jen finally speaks up. "Michael, you said we should apply this not just to our meetings but to the meetings we have with our direct reports?"

Michael nods in agreement.

Kim is unconvinced. "Right; that'll work!" she says, making no effort to conceal her sarcasm.

For Alan, her tone is too much. These are the fundamentals he believes in. "But, Kim," he says, "it's up to us to make it happen."

"Exactly," David chimes in.

Michael takes charge of the agenda once again. "I want to know if you can all buy into these ground rules—if you can own them," he says. "Tell me where you stand."

David is first to speak up. "I think this is the right course of action. We've become too loosey-goosey in terms of how we're running this company. We need more discipline and this will help."

"I agree with you," says Alan.

"I'm in," says Jen.

Roger nods.

"I guess it can't hurt," Kim concedes.

As he moves forward, Michael seems slightly less assured. "While we're on the subject of changes we can make, Jen had an idea that I was a little hesitant to bring up, but I think it could send the right message. It has to do with cutting costs. Jen had some issues with our executive dining room—she thinks it sends the wrong message, particularly when we've announced that we're going to eliminate $50 million in additional expenses over the next year."

As Michael sits down, he seems to be bracing himself for the storm.

In no time, Kim responds. "Now wait a minute," she says, tapping her index finger on the table. "I spend thirteen hours a day here. The dining room saves me time because, when things get hectic, it's a quiet place to retreat to; I can get my work done in there. Also, I'm a more productive team player because of the time I get to spend with you in there. And excuse me for saying so, but I think we've earned this perk!"

Alan understands where she's coming from, but he warms to the idea of demonstrating their commitment to change early on. "We've cut hundreds of people in the last year," Alan tells the team. "We've upset families. God only knows what they think of us, with our fancy offices and our executive chef."

His remarks meet dead silence.

Michael steps in. "Let's move on," he says. "I'd like us to hear from Jen about her experience changing corporate culture. Let's put this one aside for now."

"I'll vote for that!" Roger jokes. Everyone laughs. The tension is gone for now.

"This took longer than I expected," Michael says to Jen. "I've cut into your time. Maybe you can get started today and we'll finish on Friday."

"That's fine, Michael," Jen assures him. "I've learned the best place to start is with an understanding of our current corporate culture."

"What Jen is talking about," Alan offers, "is culture—the way we do things around here."

"Thank you, Alan, that's exactly what I mean. I've learned that culture eats strategy for lunch! What that means is that we, as leaders, get things done through our people. Execution of strategy and initiatives is all about how motivated people are to give their very best to achieve desired outcomes and results. If we don't have a culture where employees want to give their best, it doesn't matter how well-crafted our vision and strategy are—we won't achieve them. Our job as leaders is to ***create a business environment where people want to volunteer their very best.*** It's what the behavioral psychologists call ***'discretionary effort:' 'want-to' versus 'have-to' behavior.*** At my previous company, in order to establish a baseline, prioritize our efforts, and be able to measure progress, we conducted a culture audit; we used a short online survey to accomplish this. In the end, we had a clear view of where we stood in terms of employee attitudes and behaviors. Not only did we get a corporate report, but each business unit got a report indicating the current state of its culture."

"Excuse me for asking, Jen," Kim says, "but how much is something like this going to cost us? Aren't we sending a bad message by spending money on a bunch of surveys? Next, you're going to tell us we have to hire another consultant, am I right?"

Roger speaks up. "I have to agree with Kim," he says. "I'm not sure I get it."

"Oh, I get it all right," Kim says hotly. "I just think it's a waste of time and money!"

"One of our problems around here," David says to the group, "is that we try to fix things before we understand what the true nature of the problem is. We try to come up with solutions without knowing the real problem or the causes of the problem. I'd like to hear more about the potential financial gain of focusing on this culture thing. Jen, could you say more about that, based on your previous experience?"

Kim folds her arms and leans back in her chair.

Jen turns to the team: "What percentage of our current employees do you believe are volunteering discretionary effort every day: want-to versus have-to behavior?"

Roger answers her first. "We're lucky if we have 5% of our people doing that," he says.

"I think we should give people a little bit more credit," Alan says to him, "but I would say it's no more than 40-50%."

David is less optimistic. "Realistically, I think it's less than 30%."

After a heavy sigh, Michael tells them, "I can remember a time when almost everyone here worked that way."

Jen picks things up again. "Let's say it's 50%. That means that 50% of the employees at our company are not giving their full potential, not volunteering their very best. The key question we need to ask ourselves is how much does that cost us on an annual basis in terms of lost productivity, not to mention the impact it has on customer service, quality and so on."

"We know for a fact," Michael says, "that a number of our customer service reps have been bad-mouthing H&O to our customers. The impact of this and everything else you've highlighted Jen, such as lost productivity, could be in the millions of dollars!"

Alan agrees with his assessment: "Easily."

Michael turns to Jen. "I'm sold," he tells her. "Get things moving on that culture audit you talked about."

Kim is still less than enthusiastic. "I just want to go on record saying that I'm not convinced that this is the right thing to do, particularly given the recent lay-offs. It sounds very risky to me and I'm just not convinced it's a good use of our money. I think we're setting ourselves up for more bad news."

"I'll tell you what," Jen answers. "Auditing the whole company will take weeks. We could do a flash audit of our top 200 leaders and get some quick data. I've done it this way before, and I can tell you that if those results are bad, we'll know we're dealing with more severe problems in the rest of the organization. With your permission, Michael, I'd like to call the consultant we worked with at my last company. I'll find out if Brian and his team can get something done for us this week. In the meantime, I can draft a cover letter to the survey for your sig-nature—it'll let people know the purpose of the survey and assure everyone of confidentiality."

As Jen finishes, Kim mumbles, "I knew we'd be hiring another consultant!"

"That would be great," Michael says to Jen. "Now, would someone please write down the meeting ground rules and e-mail them to the rest of the team?" Alan volunteers.

"Thank you, Alan," Michael says. "Next Monday when we meet, I'd like to hear from everyone on how we're doing living by our meeting rules. Jen, I'd also like you to be ready to report on the audit results at that meeting."

Michael thanks everyone and adjourns the meeting—on time! He asks Roger to stay to discuss setting up a meeting with their largest customer.

Kim leaves the room in a hurry.

As they collect their things and prepare to leave the room, David leans over to Jen and says, conspiratorially, "Well it didn't take you long to find the deep end of the pool." Alan hears this and laughs as he joins them. "But, seriously, Jen," Alan says, "if there's anything we can do to help with the survey, just let us know."

Alan and David prepare to leave the room and as they pass Michael, David reaches over to touch Michael's shoulder. Jen sees this gesture of support. When Roger and Michael finish their conversation, Jen asks Michael if he has a minute. "I just want to thank you for listening to me, first Friday afternoon and again this morning," she tells him. "I know it isn't comfortable to hear the things that I've been saying and I know that change is not easy. One thing I learned from my mentor, Brian, is that *'it's not about perfection, it's about progress.' And I know you see that we're all going to have to be patient with one another. At times it will seem as though we're taking two steps forward, then one step backward.* What's exciting to me is that you took a big step today toward making this a better company. You put us on the path, now it's up to all of us to keep it going. I especially liked the fact that you were direct in spelling out your expectations of the team with regard to using the ground rules. You were passionate and you engaged the team in creating them. Also, you were decisive in authorizing me to engage the consultant and begin the culture audit."

Michael thanks Jen. Back in his office, he calls Edward and leaves a voice mail reporting how well things are going and how much positive change Jen is initiating. He lets him know they'll be surveying top management and will have results at the end of the week. He also tells Edward that he and Roger are setting up a meeting with their biggest customer, Fargo, Inc., who is threatening to take their business elsewhere.

Later that day, Michael gets an e-mail reply from Edward: "Thanks. I'm anxious to hear about your meeting and to see the culture survey results."

That evening, Jen tells Ted that her lunch with her assistant, Rose, went well. She had a chance to spell out her expectations for Rose, to get to know her better, and to learn about her assistant's observations concerning life at H&O. "Rose is one of those people who have been with the company forever and I'm really impressed that she's still loyal. She has seen it all—including the downward spiral—and she even lost her boss. According to Rose, Richard was a really good guy. She wouldn't say anything bad about the company, but she did warn me to watch my back, that people don't like change around here. She said that's one of the reasons Richard is gone. The amazing thing is that Rose understands Horton & Oliver's problems, maybe better than most people. You know what she told me? She said we took our eyes off people—not just our customers, but our employees, too."

Week Two, Tuesday

Jen and Michael share the elevator Tuesday morning. "I talked to Brian yesterday," she tells him. "He can start the culture audit today. I spoke with your assistant and have scheduled a meeting for the three of us on Friday afternoon so he can go over the results with us."

Kim brings the meeting rules to her own team at their Tuesday morning meeting. She had them printed up on pocket-sized cards and laminated for each of her direct reports. As she's handing them out, one man sniggers. Kim is taken aback by what she hears him say under his breath to the man at his side: "'Open and honest communication?' What—and get fired?" Kim pretends not to have heard him and continues with the meeting.

That night she wakes up angry and can't get back to sleep. It's 3:00 a.m. and she is replaying the overheard remark in her mind. Her first thought: "That guy is a real jerk."

Her second thought is more troubling: "Was he talking about me?"

Finalized Meeting Ground Rules
For
Horton & Oliver

- *Start on time and end on time*
- *Turn cell phones off*
- *Have a detailed agenda—identify discussion and decision items*
- *Distribute agenda before meetings*
- *Read agenda and prepare for meetings in advance*
- *Focus on how the discussion relates to the customer*
- *Have open and honest communication*
- *Listen for understanding*
- *Conclude meetings by reviewing action items and responsibilities*
- *Speak with one voice*

Your Turn: Be a *Change Agent*

1. If fewer than 100% of your employees are giving discretionary effort—"want-to" versus "have-to" behavior—what do you suppose is the impact on your bottom line? What impact might it have on the face your company or organization shows its customers?

2. What is it about your company's or organization's culture that is inhibiting people from volunteering discretionary effort? How are you and your leadership team influencing this behavior?

3. How different are the new Horton & Oliver ground rules (p. 29) from the way your team operates? What is the impact on your team's efficiency and effectiveness?

4. How can "open and honest communication" be offered without being offensive to those on the team?

5. Does "speak with one voice" mean that everyone is in total agreement? When it doesn't, how is disagreement handled on your team?

Culture change begins at the top.

CHAPTER 4

▼

FACING FACTS

"A problem well stated is a problem half solved."
—Charles F. Kettering

Friday, Jen and Brian meet for lunch and Brian has the survey results of H&O's top 200 leaders. First, Jen brings him up to speed on Horton & Oliver. Later, at 2:00 p.m., they are shown into Michael's office by his assistant. Michael comes out from behind his desk to offer Brian a warm greeting. "I hear you worked wonders at Jen's previous company," Michael says. He turns to Jen as he asks: "So, how bad is it?"

"Honestly, Michael, Brian hasn't shared the results with me. We're going to hear them together," Jen explains.

Michael takes a deep breath and ushers them over to his conference table where all three sit down. The report includes not only the results of the audit, but also a proposed plan and time line for addressing the issues it raises.

At the end of the meeting with Brian, Michael e-mails the results to Edward and asks for time on Edward's calendar Monday to discuss them. He adds: "The meeting with Fargo, Inc., gave new meaning to the term 'brutally honest.' But the good news is that we're talking. I assured Harry that changes are being made. We haven't lost them—at least not yet."

Michael plans to give the team the audit headlines at their 5:00 p.m. cocktail hour. The culture audit measures responses to thirty cultural statements. Of those thirty, seven triggered responses strong enough to register in the red or danger zone:

- People do not understand our mission, vision, strategy, and goals.

- We are not customer and quality driven in all that we do.

- We are not skilled at executing strategies and initiatives.

- Senior leaders do not model our values.

- People do not work as one team.

- We are not open and honest with each other.

- People do not feel appreciated and valued.

Michael shakes his head. It wasn't so long ago that employees—especially the expanded leadership team—were proud to work at H&O. Now, few, if any, employees seem happy. Things didn't improve as he went through the audit, either. Everything else in the audit showed up in the yellow or "caution" zone. Not one response landed in the green or "healthy" zone. In other words, there were no positive statements about Horton & Oliver that the top two hundred leaders agreed with wholeheartedly.

At 5:00 p.m., Michael arrives at the meeting and explains that he has to leave early for a business dinner. He just wants to give them the highlights (or lowlights) of the survey. He takes the opportunity to thank Jen again for working with Brian to make this happen so quickly. Michael points out that there is a copy of Brian's latest book for each team member on the table and calls it "good reading."

"You'll have a chance to meet Brian when we discuss his report at our Monday morning meeting," Michael tells them. He then hands out copies of the results from the culture survey of H&O's top two hundred leaders. "The bad news," he says, "is that we had nothing in the green or 'healthy' zone. Everything that wasn't labeled 'caution' was in the danger zone and there are seven of those. The lowest average score was in the area of being customer and quality driven."

Just as Michael's ready to continue, Edward puts his head in the door of the Boardroom. "Michael, may we have a word?"

Michael turns to the group and tells them to have a good weekend.

Edward leads Michael into Michael's office. "I'm glad your meeting with Harry and his team at Fargo went well," he says, "but the real reason I'm here is to talk to you about those culture audit results. It would be an understatement to say that those results concern me. As I see it, the only good news is that we're conducting these surveys and we're finding out how bad things really are. What I want to make clear is that your legacy, the imprint you leave on this company, is being determined now, by how successful you are in turning the opinions of our employees around. After all, they're the ones who provide service to our customers!"

"The Board is growing very weary, but they will stand behind you. But time is of the essence. Get this done and get it done now. Based on what you've told me, it sounds as though Jen has a lot of experience in this area. Use that experience. Let her help you with this. People associate you with Horton & Oliver, but don't let your pride keep you from listening to a new perspective."

Edward leans in to shake Michael's hand before leaving and adds, "Just get it done!"

Michael walks out to his assistant. "I need you to set up a meeting with Alan for Monday. Please let him know I want him to talk about closing the executive dining room. And please cancel the flowers for next week. We have a new policy. We won't be spending money on flowers for the building anymore."

Once the doors on the elevator have closed and Michael is headed downstairs, his assistant says aloud to herself: "Well, what do you know! Things may be beginning to change around here!"

Your Turn: Become the *Change Agent*

1. Before you can begin a journey of any kind you have to know where you are. At the end of Chapter 1, you described the current culture of your company or organization. What kind of data do you have that confirms (or refutes) your assessment?

2. If you were to conduct a culture audit of your company or organization, what areas of strength and opportunities for improvement do you think would be revealed?

3. What is the impact of your company's or organization's current culture—as reflected in the data—on execution and results?

4. From the standpoint of accountability, how have you contributed to your company's or organization's culture? Based on what you know now, what will you do differently?

Prescription without diagnosis is malpractice.

PART II

Setting a New Course

CHAPTER 5

▼

TAKING OWNERSHIP

"When you have decided what you believe in, what you feel must be done, have the courage to stand and be counted."
—*Eleanor Roosevelt*

Jen and Ted have the house to themselves Saturday and decide to sleep in. There is nothing on the calendar except for a dinner party that evening, so they have the day to work in the garden, take a bike ride or just relax. They're still in bed reading the paper at 9:30 a.m. when the doorbell rings. Ted gets up, puts on his robe and goes to the door. It's the local florist with a bouquet of fresh flowers. They're for Jen, from Michael. Ted brings the flowers upstairs. There is a thank-you note tucked into the basket on which Michael has hand-written: "Thank you for adding so much value in such a short amount of time. I'll be relying on you as we turn H&O around. P.S. I paid for the flowers myself!" Jen smiles and passes the card to Ted. He smiles. "Looks like you're off to a great start in your new job, Jen. I'm happy for you."

Jen is up quite early Sunday morning, getting in an hour or so of work before the day begins. Her son is due home at lunch time. He's asked for her help picking out a new sofa and rug for his apartment. She's looking forward to spending time with him. He lives less than an hour away, but she misses seeing him every day.

After finishing her business correspondence, Jen sends Michael an e-mail thanking him for the flowers, but, more especially, for his kind words. Jen adds that she's looking forward to supporting his efforts.

Week Three, Monday

Monday morning, the team gathers at 8:00 a.m. Additional copies of the agenda are on the conference table. Roger makes a show of shutting off his cell phone. The others quietly check theirs. After fighting unbelievable traffic, Kim rushes into the room just as the clock strikes 8:00 a.m. David stands up and applauds. Kim shoots him a sour look and says, "You're a real comedian, David!" David is quick to respond: "Don't take it personally, Kim. I was actually applauding the entire team. This is a first for us."

Kim catches her breath and calmly takes her seat. Jen turns to Brian and says, "Remember I told you on Friday about the meeting ground rules that we've adopted. This is a start."

Michael's first remarks are addressed to Brian: "In just a minute we'll do introductions, but I want to thank you for making time to meet with me Friday and coming back today to talk about the results of the audit and potential next steps. I'm sure everyone here has read your report."

After going around the table so everyone on the team can introduce himself/herself, Michael turns things over to Brian.

"As you know, we've begun a culture audit of the entire company, starting with the top two hundred leaders," Brian tells them. "It will take about three weeks for my team to complete the audit of the entire company and assemble the results."

During the next hour, he presents and explains the results of the audit of H&O's top two hundred leaders, taking questions as he goes. Kim is shocked to find so little satisfaction among this group—what can the results be like for the rest of Horton & Oliver? As they talk over the results with Brian, she and her colleagues gradually recover from the bad news and begin to look for ways to turn things around. As he wraps up, Brian compliments the team on what he's seen as an open, candid discussion.

Michael turns to Brian and says: "In your book, you talk about the journey of culture change. The plan you've proposed calls for taking the executive team off site for a two-day retreat. Did you do that at your company, Jen?"

"Yes," she answers. "I have to say it's a vital part of the culture-change process."

Brian begins to talk about the change process beginning at the top. He turns to Jen and asks: "Have you introduced the principle of 'employees mirroring the behaviors of their leaders?'"

Jen nods, "That's how this whole process began."

Brian smiles and makes eye contact with each team member as he scans the room. "That's wonderful. It sounds as though you've been trying out some new behaviors in the past week that have to do with meeting management and dynamics. How has that been working?"

Kim speaks up first: "It's been painful. But I'm making some slow progress with my team."

"It's been a week since we established these ground rules," Michael says, "and we've gotten progressively better with each meeting. Today is our best yet. This feels good!"

"Change is tough," Alan adds. "But I like what I'm seeing so far."

Roger sighs. "In Sales, it's still like herding cats."

David is empathetic. "Give it time. Just continue to model the behavior you want and keep letting people know you expect the same from them."

Brian moves the discussion forward. "So what do you think the impact of these changes has been on people and productivity?"

"It's clearly better," David says. "We're getting more done and we're being more respectful of people's time. Respecting people is, if I remember correctly, one of our core values."

This prompts Brian to ask: "By the way, what are your core values? I haven't seen them anywhere."

The pause that follows the question almost becomes embarrassing. Alan breaks the silence. "C'mon guys. Our values are respect, integrity…"

Kim finishes the list, "and excellence."

Jen has been listening and asks the group: "Have you taken those values and behavioralized them? In other words, have you spelled out how you expect people to behave when it comes to each value?"

"Good question," Alan says, nodding thoughtfully. "Not really. We list them on the form we use for our annual performance reviews, but there are no objective measures. I guess we haven't really defined them in terms of what behaviors we expect. We've spent more time defining the technical competencies needed to do particular jobs."

Kim is more enthusiastic. "Well let me tell you what I've done in my group. I've had the meeting ground rules put on laminated cards for each person and had posters made up for our conference room."

"Good for you, Kim!" Michael says.

Brian has been listening. "What you've done are key and useful antecedents in the process of change."

On behalf of the team, Roger asks, "What's an antecedent?"

"An antecedent is a prompt," Brian answers. *"It's what gets desired behaviors going. For example, telling people what you expect from them and then giving them the training and tools they need to be successful—these are antecedents.* Another would be to behavioralize the values and then communicate them to the work force so everyone will know how to behave. Kim, the posters and the laminated cards are two good examples of antecedents. Good job! *Antecedents like these are a key part of the change process."*

"Maybe we should all do that," Michael suggests. "Maybe we should put our meeting ground rules in all the conference rooms."

Everyone nods in agreement. Kim volunteers to take care of getting this done. David thanks her and Michael congratulates the group on their teamwork.

Next, Brian puts up a slide with the heading "Inside-Out & Outside-In Change Methodology." "One of the things that we have to do," he tells the team, "is *unfreeze existing beliefs that are getting in the way of desired performance—this is the 'inside-out' piece.* Then we need *to reinforce the behaviors that are helpful to us and correct those that aren't helpful—this is the 'outside-in' piece.* Organizational *culture change begins with personal change.* An executive retreat, if you decide to have one, is about beginning or continuing the process of personal change within the context of leading organizational change. I'll let it go at that. I've learned that it's better not to say too much before a retreat. I know that flies in the face of the importance of having an agenda, and I have to ask your forgiveness for breaking one of your ground rules. What I've learned from experience is that it's more productive this way. The primary reason for this is that we may need to make a course correction during the retreat to address the needs of the team versus stick to a defined agenda"

Michael has been listening intently. "I like what I've heard so far. We're going to take the time and commit to doing this. Jen, will you work with Brian and make this happen as quickly as possible?

"And, I need to address two more things before we adjourn our meeting. First, you may have noticed this morning that there aren't any fresh flowers on the executive floor. In the spirit of setting a good example regarding spending, I've made that easy change. The other change I've decided to make was more difficult. I want to thank Alan for helping me with it earlier today. I've decided to close the executive dining room. My expectation is that each of us, when we're in the building, will dine in the employee cafeteria. I think it would be good for us to *spend more time with our employees, our colleagues. We need to not just be visible, but to engage them in conversation and find out what's on their minds."*

Kim, clearly taken by surprise by the announcement, speaks up. "Don't we have to be careful about how we do that? We don't want to come across as if we're spying on them or launching some new PR campaign!"

Brian answers her. "That's a good point, Kim. We can talk more about that at the retreat. In the meantime, follow *the first rule of leadership: 'be authentic.'* *When you're in the cafeteria, be yourself."*

Kim shrugs, then looks at Brian and says, "That's easy for you to say—you don't know our employees!"

In the days leading up to the retreat, the members of the executive team complete a different survey on their effectiveness as a team. In addition, Brian interviews each member individually for about an hour. In these interviews, they discuss the challenges facing the company, the strengths and weaknesses of the team, etc. In his book, Brian refers to this as the data-gathering component of his **5D Methodology**, which stands for **D**ata gathering, **D**iagnosis, **D**esign, **D**elivery, and **D**etermination of impact (i.e., measurement).

At the same time, team members notice improvement in the effectiveness of their meetings—in the Boardroom and with their staffs. The impact of having lunch in the cafeteria takes a bit longer to develop. At first, the team members are a bit uneasy. They stick together for awhile, then, as employees begin returning their smiles, they relax and ask permission to join employees for lunch. The good news is that discussions are lively and helpful.

Before long, members of the executive team realize they have much in common with the employees. For their part, the employees warm to the idea of being listened to and begin to open up. At Kim's suggestion, the executive team starts asking for input. They ask employees to tell them the number one thing they'd like to see changed at Horton & Oliver and to name the biggest obstacle to accomplishing that change.

Week Four, The Retreat

Despite making some early contributions to H&O's culture-change effort, Kim is not looking forward to the retreat; she sees it as a necessary evil. She decides she might as well make the best of it. Brian stressed the value of getting the team away from the office so they could focus on the work that needs to be done and everyone agreed. Consequently, Michael has arranged free space at his country club for the retreat.

The big day finally arrives. Michael welcomes the team. He tells them that he and Brian met for breakfast that morning. Michael says he's excited about the opportunity to learn and grow as individual leaders and as a team, given the major challenges that are facing them regarding turning around the organization.

"The focus of this retreat," Michael says, turning to Brian, "and correct me if I'm wrong, is to work at three levels: individual, team, and organizational. This means that we'll be focusing on personal leadership and teamwork within the context of our corporate culture work.

"As you can see," he says, gesturing to the room they're in, "there are no tables in the room, just chairs, so we're sitting here kind of exposed. I have to admit, I'm a little bit uncomfortable; but, Brian has assured me that everything will be fine."

These remarks are met with a bit of grumbling.

"More room for group hugs," Kim groans.

"Where am I supposed to put my coffee?" Roger wonders aloud.

"Is this going to be like group therapy?" David asks Brian.

Alan says, "I hope you're not going to have us do any 'trust falls'—I'm not sure we have enough corporate insurance!"

Hearing their nervous laughter, Michael gets ready to turn the floor over to Brian; but first, he reviews the team's meeting ground rules and asks that everyone follows them.

Brian greets the team and pauses a moment to compliment Michael on doing a nice job of setting the stage for the retreat. Then, Brian asks permission to add an item to the team's meeting ground rules. "One of the things that will allow us to optimize our time together over the next two days is if each of us commits to *be in the moment. Not only must we be present physically, but also we each have to commit to be here mentally, to focus on the work at hand.*" Brian continues, "How many of you, already this morning, have found your mind drifting off to things back at work or somewhere else?" Laughter erupts as everyone raises his or her hand.

"What is the impact of 'drifting off' when it comes to getting things accomplished at meetings, etc.?" he asks.

David responds, "It's simple. Everything takes longer to do."

Michael adds: "When I'm mentally distracted, I lose focus and often miss what's being said. This hurts discussions and decision making."

Brian says: "You're both right. So, for the next two days, I'm going to ask you to *practice being in the moment.* If you find your mind wandering, please refocus your attention or ask for a break. We'll be taking breaks every seventy-five minutes or so to help us stay focused on our mission."

"One final thing about being in the moment," Brian says, "is that it's a key leadership principle. For example, when it comes to H&O's value of respect, one of the most powerful ways I can demonstrate respect for others is by being 'fully present' for them as we're talking."

Brian sees everyone nodding in agreement, so he chooses to move on by discussing the focus of the retreat.

He reiterates what Michael has said earlier, that their focus is on individual and team leadership within the context of organizational change. "I'm referring to, among other things," he tells them, "changing or transforming the culture of this organization."

"Before we jump into it, one of the things that I think is ***most important in any change process is to acknowledge and celebrate successes along the way,*** even if some people would call those successes 'baby steps.' So, what I'd like you to do now is turn to the person sitting next to you and share any success stories that you've observed or been part of since I saw you almost two weeks ago."

After the bad news the team received from the results of the culture audit, Kim is relieved to start the retreat with something positive. She tells Roger about a positive discussion she had with her assistant about getting meeting agendas out ahead of time.

Around the room, the conversations are tentative at first, but not for long. After ten minutes, Brian calls the group back together, saying: "The energy level in the room has just gone up significantly. I'm anxious to hear what you shared with your partner."

The first to speak is Alan, who says that he and David, who were paired, talked about the positive impact the meeting ground rules have had on focus, efficiency, and productivity. "It's been really great," he says, "bringing our focus back to the customer."

"At our level—and my direct reports tell me it's happening in their staff meetings, too—agendas are going out in advance of meetings and people are coming prepared."

"Yeah," David interrupts, "and some of the politeness is starting to wear off. I think that's a good thing. What I mean is that I can see that soon we'll start to debate and challenge one another. I think it would be really healthy for all of us. God knows I'm trying to stimulate some of that!"

Jen agrees: "Having the ground rules posted in conference rooms has been great reinforcement. They're a positive reminder of how we want to run our meetings."

"I really like the concept of keeping the focus on the customer," Roger adds. "We actually cancelled a meeting the other day because it had nothing to do with the customer and we realized we weren't clear why we were meeting in the first place. I was just telling Kim, it felt good to cancel one of these meetings." Kim turns to Roger and gives him a high-five.

Michael is obviously pleased. "Good for you, Roger! I agree that our meetings have been more focused and more effective. But let's remember that this is just a start."

"You're right, Michael," Brian tells him. "Just remember, *people in this organization pay attention to what you pay attention to. If you care about the customer and the quality of meetings, they will care about those things, too.*"

"That's helpful, Brian," Michael says. "I think eating meals in the cafeteria is starting to have a positive impact, too."

Kim nods her head. "Last week I sat down at a table and for the first time, everyone didn't get up and walk away!" She laughs. "It wasn't <u>that</u> bad before, but I do see a difference."

"I'm even learning something, Kim," says David. "That question you suggested we ask about the number one thing that could be improved at H&O to make it an even better company, I think that was a great idea and I'm starting to hear some common themes emerge."

"Like what, David?" Jen asks.

"Well, you know I'm a heavy diet soda drinker," David answers, "so I probably spend more time in the cafeteria than some of the rest of you. When I see a group of people, I sit down and ask them about what's happening in their lives."

"Are you saying you've been doing more listening than talking?" Brian asks.

"That's exactly right," David says. "Eventually I asked the question: 'What would make this an even better company?'"

"At first, people were really reluctant to answer. I don't think they trusted that I was really interested in their opinions. But there was this one guy who blew me away. He said, 'I'll probably get fired for saying this, but you guys at the top don't know how to listen to the people doing the job.'"

The others in the room are listening closely to David. "This guy said that as much as we count on them, he thought we ought to listen once in awhile. Finally, he said: 'You're paying me to do a job here. Give me the tools I tell you I need and then get out of my way. I'll get the job done, if you let me.'"

David goes on. "More than one person felt that way and took the time to talk to me about it. We seem to have taken our eyes off the employees. People don't feel valued. They don't feel appreciated for the contributions they make. And they sure don't feel listened to. They don't feel like they have a voice in the process, even though they're the process experts when it comes to doing their specific jobs. To me, it sounds as though we've become very hierarchical, with things driven from the top down. Years ago, we used to empower our people to suggest improvements and to make decisions. It seems as though we've lost that focus."

"Well, how do we fix that?" Kim asks, turning to Brian.

"That's a great question, Kim," Brian says. "Let's create a 'parking lot' of issues that we want to be sure to come back to later." Alan volunteers and writes "How to value employees?" on the flipchart. "There are some other things I want us to do before we go there," Brian says. "Is there anything else that is worthy of celebration before we move on?"

"I know I'm the new kid on the block, but I've been through this type of change process before," Jen tells them. "I want to compliment the members of this team for beginning *the process of looking in the mirror to determine what more we can do to turn this company around and for starting with changing ourselves.*"

Kim looks at her thoughtfully, "You are the new kid, but it seems like you've been here for a long time!"

Roger jumps in, "Want to explain that? That could be a good thing or a bad thing!"

"I think it's a little of both," Kim says quietly.

"Well, Kim, we'll have an opportunity to explore what you meant by that a little later this morning," Brian tells her. "Before we move on, I want to commend you on the great start you've made in the past few weeks. Based on past experience, you're ahead of the curve already, compared to other organizations in a similar place. Congratulate one another." Team members turn to each other, smile and shake hands all around.

The conversation continues. While no one else on the team heard from anyone quite as candid as the man David spoke with, each one has a story to tell. They all seem to follow the same theme: management has lost touch with the work going on in the trenches.

Brian suggests this as he calls the group to order. "I want to get back to what David was talking about. He was describing the organizational culture of H&O. Anyone want to tell me what I mean by organizational culture?"

For the next hour or so, after defining *corporate culture as learned behavior, resulting from organizational beliefs, biases, traditions, values, rewards, punishments, etc.,* the group discusses the power of culture and how it can support or derail business execution. They talk about the fact that employees mirror the behaviors of their leaders; therefore, senior leaders have a major impact on shaping organizational culture.

"If we hope to be effective leaders," Alan announces, "<u>we</u> have to do what we want our staffs to do. We have to model the values of Horton & Oliver. It's up to us to create the culture we want."

"And how would you describe that culture?" Brian asks.

"Well, it's what Jen talked about early on," says Alan, "one where people volunteer discretionary effort. It's up to us to build the workplace people **want to come to**, rather than a place they feel they **have to work**. Until we approach Horton & Oliver with energy and commitment, we can't expect our employees to; it starts with our own behavior."

"Let me suggest another way to express that," Brian says as he puts up a slide for the group to consider.

High-Performance = Desired Results + Desired Behaviors

"Anyone want to take a shot at telling us what that means?" Brian asks.

"Let me try," Michael offers. "If we want to build a high-performance culture, we need to communicate more than just the results we want. We have to communicate the behaviors we want, as well. I'd add that we have to **communicate by our actions, not just our words**."

"And since culture change begins with us," Jen adds, "It's up to each of us to make it happen. The only person I can control and truly change is myself. If I want a more effective team and organization, first I have to become a more effective contributor and leader."

"Great observation," Brian says. "Too often in a change process, our focus becomes fixing other people first, without examining our own behavior. I'm sure there would be at least 50% fewer divorces if people realized that—that **the only person you can truly change is yourself!**"

"So, our focus today is going to be on '**self as an instrument of change.**' I'd ask each of you to focus on what more you can do to improve this team and this organization's culture beginning today."

"Now let's shift gears for a moment and have some fun. I have something I'd like you to do. Let's start with the word 'seldom.' Please write down on a piece of paper the percentage of time (between 0 and 100) that word represents to you. If you want, we can use it in a sentence. Alan, I'm going to pick on you for a moment: 'Alan seldom listens to people without interrupting.' Based on that statement, what percentage of time, between 0 and 100%, would you say Alan listens to people without interrupting? Write it down. Now let's pick another word: 'frequently.' 'Alan frequently listens to people without interrupting.' What percentage of time, between 0 and 100%, does that represent to you? Write it down. Okay, show your neighbor what you wrote down for seldom and what you wrote down for frequently."

People burst into laughter and chatter as they compare their answers. Brian says, "So, what's so funny?"

Kim is first. "Well, Jen got it wrong," she laughs.

"Let's hear all the percentages," Brian says. "Let's start with seldom and go around the room quickly."

Michael says, "15%."

Kim doesn't hide her surprise, "You've got to be kidding—2%!"

Jen is next: "10%"

Alan: "25%"

"What are you thinking of?" Kim bursts out.

Roger feigns embarrassment. "I'm afraid to give my answer. You're going to hate it. I have 20%." Kim rolls her eyes.

When David says "5%," Kim exclaims, "thank you David—finally, a voice of reason!"

The group is uncomfortably quiet for a moment.

Roger turns to Kim. "Now I see why you go off when we're talking about business, Kim. Look how worked up you're getting over a stupid little activity!"

Michael is uneasy. "C'mon team," he says. "Let's **save the competition for H&O's competition.**"

"I'm sure the same thing would happen," Brian tells them, "if we went around the room with the word 'frequently.'"

Kim is quick to answer. "Spare me the pain!" she moans.

"So, what's going on here?" Brian asks, "Why all these different percentages?"

"Clearly, we all see things very differently on this team," Kim answers.

"We have different perceptions," David adds.

"We call this the **principle of separate realities**," Brian says. He takes off his glasses and holds them up to demonstrate. "**Each of us sees life through his/her own unique set of lenses. This is based on life experiences, values, beliefs, biases, the parenting we experienced growing up**—I could go on and on. I've done this activity a hundred times. It's not surprising that people come up with very different answers for commonly used words. So, how many of you, maybe in that activity that we just did or in life, believe that your reality is the correct one?"

Everyone laughs, but Kim speaks up, "C'mon, guys! Sometimes you do have the wrong answers."

"Kim," Brian asks her, "do you know for a fact that 2% was or is the correct answer for the word seldom?"

The others in the room are gently kidding her as she considers her answer. "C'mon, Kim," they tease.

Kim, on the other hand, is taken aback. "Why are you all acting like jerks?"

Roger responds, perhaps a little more harshly than he realizes: "Now you know what it feels like! Five minutes ago you were criticizing all of us for the answers we came up with."

Brian steps in. "So, *there is an important lesson here, as it pertains to separate realities and leadership. That is, when a person has a different reality than ours, we have a choice: we can approach them from a place of curiosity or from a place of judgment.*" He pauses a moment before asking, "What do you think I mean by that?"

Once again, Michael answers first. "If people see something differently from the way I do," he offers, "I can either wonder why they see things differently or I can judge them as being wrong. Now that I think about it, sometimes I can become self righteous, believing that my answer or reality is correct; consequently, I judge others harshly, call them idiots or stupid—even just in my own mind—when I could have asked questions to explore why they see things the way they do."

"Good!" says Brian. "Why is it important to ask those questions, to find out why the other person sees things the way they do?"

"First of all, it's respectful. Secondly, maybe I could learn from them, learn something that I don't know," David says.

"That sounds a lot more like humility than self-righteousness," says Brian.

Alan speaks up. "This is a powerful discussion. I believe on this team, each of us," carefully eyeing Kim, "tends to believe that his or her own reality is the correct reality and we tend to judge each other and tune each other out."

"What is the impact of that when it comes to relationships and individual and team effectiveness?" Brian asks the group.

"It hurts relationships and weakens performance," Michael answers.

David says, "I agree with Alan and Michael."

"Before we go any further," Brian says, "I'd like you to pull out your workbooks; we're going to take a couple of minutes of quiet time to reflect on the discussion we've just had. I'd like you to consider this learning methodology." He puts up a slide that says:

ARC Learning Methodology:
Awareness, Reflection, and Choice

He tells them: "This is going to be the approach that guides us over the next two days. First, we're going to raise our awareness of how we behave and its impact. Then, we'll have an opportunity to reflect on why we behave the way we do—i.e., we'll focus on our beliefs or thought habits. Finally, we'll make choices about what we might want to continue doing, stop doing or perhaps start doing. At the back of your workbooks there is a section titled 'Personal Notes and Commitments.' In this section, I want you to journal answers to two questions." He moves to the easel and flips the blank page to reveal a page with two questions and reads them aloud.

---

1. What did I learn or re-learn about myself during this discussion?
2. What, if anything, will I choose to do differently?

There is quiet in the room as each person writes. When Brian notices that people have stopped writing, he asks them to partner with someone new and share what they've written. Lively discussions take place—Brian sees this as a good sign. After ten minutes, he brings closure to the one-on-one discussions and invites people to share with the large group.

"This is a tough one for me," Michael admits. "I was trained to have confidence in myself, my decisions, and my point of view. As I rose up the corporate ladder, I became more convinced that my way of seeing the world is the correct way of seeing the world. So, as I answer that first question, it has become clear to me that I don't listen to people as well as I could. I quickly draw a conclusion, form a judgment, finish someone's sentence, tune out and move on. I'm afraid my confidence has turned to arrogance. I don't feel good about that! But, going back to the way I began my remarks, I've learned to be this way over the last thirty-plus years in the business world. In terms of what I will do differently, first of all I need to become more aware of when I'm judging others because they see things differently than I do. Then I need to make a conscious choice to explore their point of view and not just dismiss it."

Brian turns to Michael and says: "So, when you go to that place of judgment and stop listening to people, do you think they know you've stopped listening?"

"Of course they do!" Michael and David answer together. Everyone laughs.

"What's amazing," Michael continues, "is that I haven't been conscious of doing this for years. It's such a simple thing, this notion of coming from curiosity versus judgment. I'm embarrassed to admit I've been totally unaware."

"Don't be so hard on yourself, Michael," Alan says. "As senior leaders, I think we've all been conditioned to believe that we always have the best answer. It seems to come with the executive job title."

"So," Brian asks, "what is the impact of that behavior on others?"

"People become frustrated," says David. "They don't feel listened to. They think that we're arrogant and that our egos are the size of this building. It turns people off, basically."

Jen adds, "And we lose their input and their creativity."

Kim speaks up, a bit tentatively. "Can I go next?" she asks. "That little activity with those words, 'seldom' and 'frequently,' really hit home with me. Particularly when I reflect on how critical I become when people disagree with me." She looks to Brian and asks: "I don't know whether I should ask your permission to do this, but I'd like to ask the team how often I come across that way?"

"Go ahead, Kim," he answers. "Ask your question of the team."

"So," she asks them, "Do I come across as a know-it-all bitch?"

Before anyone can answer, Brian says, "Kim, I'd like to help you rephrase that."

"I'll take any help I can get!" she says.

"When it comes to demonstrating curiosity rather than judgment," Brian asks the group, "how could Kim be even more effective?"

"You're good, Brian," Michael says. "That's a very positive way of asking that question."

Alan is first to answer. "Kim," he says, "first, I want to tell you I think it takes courage to ask for feedback like that in the first two hours of our retreat. It's also a little difficult for me to provide feedback because I could be more effective in this area myself. I tend to jump to conclusions and make negative assumptions about people without giving them a fair chance. But let me say I think you are one of the most intelligent and talented executives in this company. I think, to some extent, you know that. My experience of you is this—when you get your way, things go well and you're a lot better at follow through than when you don't."

There is an awkward silence. Brian turns to Kim. "What do you want to say to Alan?" he asks.

"Screw you?" Kim says sardonically.

"Try again," says Brian.

"Thank you?" Kim responds.

"That's better." says Brian. "***Feedback is a gift when the provider's intention is to help, not harm and when the impact of the feedback is helpful, not harmful.*** It's a gift because when we're doing something well, we want to know specifically what we're doing so that we can continue doing it—we call this positive feedback. When it's something we need to do differently or not at all, we need to know that too, so that we can become even more effective leaders—we call this constructive feedback. Feedback becomes negative when the provider's intention or his/her impact is harmful."

"In that case, thank you for the gift, Alan," Kim says. The group laughs.

"Kim, ol' buddy, ol' pal," says Roger, "I've got something for you. I'm not sure you want to hear it, but I have something to say. What occurred during the 'seldom' and 'frequently' activity is exactly what happens in our meetings. If people don't see things the way you do, you put them down. Because you're so damn smart, we don't challenge you. To be honest, people are intimidated by you."

Brian intervenes. "Roger, ***I'd like you to take ownership of your own feelings.*** So, let me ask you, who feels intimidated?"

"I do," Roger answers with little conviction.

"Thanks, Roger. It's important to own your own feedback," Brian says.

Brian notices a pained look on Kim's face. He looks at her and asks gently, "Kim, are you okay?"

Kim takes a deep breath and in a strong voice says: "I'm fine. This is just tough to hear. I never intended to have such a negative impact on you guys."

"Don't take all of this on your shoulders, Kim," David tells her. "I could have told you before this that your behavior is challenging at times, but I chose not to. God knows, some of my own behavior is probably challenging to you all, too!"

"So, let's see what lessons we can draw from this," Brian says, "not only you, Kim, but all of us."

"Well, as executives," Kim suggests, "just because we think we should know everything doesn't mean we do. Man, that's hard to swallow."

"Let me offer another way to put that," Brian says. "***Because each of us is living a separate reality, we have blind spots.*** That's why the old expression two heads are better than one is so valid. ***It's when we come from that place of questioning and curiosity and enter into true open dialogue that we come up with better answers, better solutions and better decisions.*** Another key lesson is that ***intention does not equal impact.*** We can be the most well-intentioned people and still have a negative impact on others because of the behavior we exhibit.

Most of the executives I know truly want to do a good job as leaders, but they are often clueless about the impact that their behavior has on employees' feeling valued, appreciated, empowered and listened to—all of those things that appeared in the culture audit.

"So, if we're going to change some of these habits or patterns of behavior, who has to change?"

"We do," the group answers him.

"I need an even more personal commitment than that," says Brian.

"I do?" Roger says tentatively.

Brian responds, "Right on, Roger! "Remember, there is only one person you can change and that's yourself. There are more lessons, but we can explore those over the next two days. It feels like it's time for a break."

"Before we go," Kim asks, "may I say something else?"

"Certainly," Brian replies.

"My God," she begins, "I didn't realize I was going to become the focal point of this morning's discussion!"

"You're doing great, Kim," Michael assures her.

"So let me tell you what I choose to do differently," she goes on. "The choice I'm making going forward is to use my energy in a positive way to collaborate, to find better solutions, to use this notion of separate realities as leverage to come up with better ideas, better solutions and better decisions."

"Based on my limited time here," says Jen, "if you and the rest of us commit to doing that, I think that would go a long way to making this a great team."

"Here, here!" Michael chimes in.

"Let's take a 15-minute break," says Brian.

When the group reassembles, Brian starts things off. "Let me share a model with you that I believe is appropriate, given the discussion that we had prior to the break. We said earlier that each of us is living a separate reality, based on the different lenses and perceptions through which we look at life. One of the most powerful lenses through which we look at the world is our beliefs." He pauses and puts up a new slide, titled "Understanding Human Behavior." "When an event occurs in our life," Brian explains, "it is filtered through the lens of our beliefs. When I talk about beliefs, I'm talking about some ingrained thought patterns that we have—a thought habit. ***Our beliefs drive our behaviors.*** Our behaviors produce results and other consequences that either reinforce the belief that started this cycle or challenge it. So, for example, if I have a belief that there isn't enough time in the day to do my job—if that's my belief, that my job is too big, that I don't have enough time to do it all during the course of a nine- or ten-hour work day—what might be my behavior resulting from that belief?"

"Well, if it were me," Alan answers. "I might start cutting some corners."

"What would be the consequence of that?" Brian asks the group.

"The consequence might be that you would make more mistakes and have to do rework," says Michael.

"And what belief would that reinforce?" replies Brian.

"It would reinforce the belief that started the whole cycle, that I don't have enough time to do my work in the course of a normal business day," answers Kim.

Brian shares: "As Ernest Holmes once said, 'Life is a mirror and will reflect back to the thinker what he or she thinks into it.' Another one of my favorite sayings that I learned from a dear colleague is, *'My relationship with you can only be as good as the conversation I have about you in my mind.'"*

Understanding Human Behavior

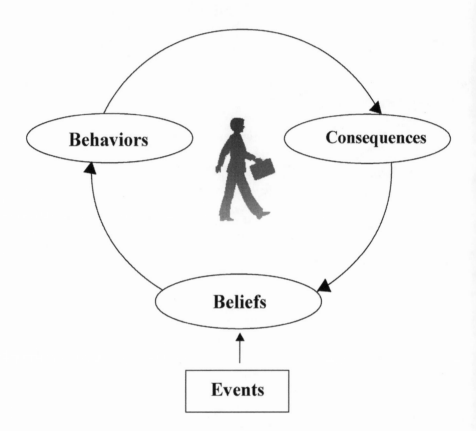

"I'll say that one again, *'My relationship with you can only be as good as the conversation I have about you in my mind.'* So, the bottom line is, our thinking plays a major role in our lives because our beliefs or thought habits drive our behaviors.

Going back to what we were discussing just before the break, when I accept a thought—perhaps a negative thought about someone or something—and believe it's true without inquiry, I'm living my life on what I call autopilot." Brian shows a new slide. It reads:

HOW DO I LEAD?

> ***With Judgment:***
> - Leave autopilot on
> - Assume "my truth" is "The Truth"
> - Find person "guilty"
> - Get frustrated or angry
> - Hold a grudge

OR

> ***With Curiosity and Empathy:***
> - Turn off autopilot
> - Am curious
> - Put myself in other person's shoes
> - Assume the best
> - Forgive

"We've talked about choosing to listen differently, from a place of curiosity," Brian says. He moves to the flip chart and finds a blank page. "Let's put that another way: Given H&O's stated value of respect, it's really about respecting other people's opinions. So, instead of automatically rejecting an idea because it's different than yours, I'll call this 'behaving on autopilot,'" He stops to write on the page:

> ***Stimulus → Response (Automatic Response = Autopilot)***

"You stop and truly listen to the idea from a place of curiosity and then choose your response." Brian then writes:

> ***Stimulus → Pause and Choose → Response***

"Let's link this to the ARC Learning Methodology that we discussed earlier. Personal change starts with becoming more aware of our thought and behavior habits, and their impact on others. Learning to pause and reflect, and then choosing a response that will have the desired impact is what it's all about." He continues: "Remember that employees mirror the behaviors of their leaders. So, if I routinely operate on autopilot, for example, by quickly and harshly judging other people's ideas, I am sending a powerful message to the troops that that's acceptable behavior. Remember, when it comes to culture change, who has the greatest impact?"

"I do!" they answer in unison.

"Excellent. Whom can you change?" he asks the team.

"Myself!" they say together.

"Good," Brian says. "So, remember what George Bernard Shaw said: 'Progress is impossible without change, and those who cannot change their minds cannot change anything.' Again, it comes back to using yourself as an instrument of change."

"You know, Brian," Alan says, "you've got me thinking about a lot of things here, but at the end of the day, isn't this simply common sense; I mean there's really nothing new or earth-shattering here."

"*It is common sense*," Brian answers. "*The problem is that it's not put into common practice!*"

For the rest of that day and into the next one, the team continues on the path of self discovery within the context of leading organizational culture change. One of the key moments of the retreat occurs on the morning of day two when the team is discussing the difference between accountable and unaccountable behavior. Brian puts up a slide:

Accountability = Attitude of <u>Ownership</u>
Ask yourself: "If I owned this company, what would I do?"

He explains that accountability begins as an attitude, an attitude of ownership. "In other words," he asks them, "if you owned this company, how would you behave on a daily basis? What decisions would you make? What decisions would you challenge? What more would you do to use yourself as an instrument of change? When it comes to day-to-day behavior, being unaccountable often sounds like whining or complaining." The next slide follows up on his point:

Being unaccountable sounds like:

> "It's not my job."
> "No one ever tells me anything."
> "They did it!"
> "If only s/he would…"
> "Let someone else do it for a change."
> "All I get around here is useless advice."

Being accountable sounds like:

> "What more can I do?"
> "How can I support you?"
> "What's best for the organization/team?"
> "I accept responsibility for what happened."
> "I will coach him/her."
> "Please coach me."

Brian leads the team through an activity. He asks them to answer the question: "If I owned Horton & Oliver, what is the number one thing I would change immediately to improve this company?" They write in their workbooks individually. Then Brian asks them to pair up with someone with whom they haven't yet worked. After they've had time to discuss their answers one-on-one, Brian asks for group input.

Kim is paired with Alan and, perhaps for the first time, realizes his strengths as an HR professional. She's impressed with the way he listens to her suggestions and is careful about phrasing his own. She encourages him to speak up.

"The first thing I would change," Alan says to the team, "is our communication with our employees. Since our financials have gone downhill, we spend a lot of time talking among ourselves, but, with the exception of the last few weeks, we spend little time in conversation with employees. I'd like to see us conduct town hall meetings where we talk about the current state of the company and our vision for the future, as well as our plans to get there. In fact, instead of just talking at them, we should engage them in open dialogue so we get their input on these things, too. That would send a powerful message around here." The others nod in agreement.

David adds: "We've been asking people when we have lunch in the cafeteria what they think about this question since Kim suggested it. But we've only taken a few baby steps in that area. I agree with you, Alan, that communication is key. But before we can do that, we have to be clear in this room where we're taking this company and how we're going to get there strategically, as well as tactically."

"So," says Michael, "what I'm hearing the two of you say is that doing some new work around vision and strategic planning would be helpful, as well as creating a new communication plan. In addition to focusing more effort on employees, what I wrote down is that we need to focus on communication with our customers, too. I'm talking about basic, face-to-face communication with our best customers—no, now that I think of it, with all of our current and potential customers, even with former customers—to begin getting our relationships back to where they used to be. Horton & Oliver was founded on having fantastic relationships with our customers and employees. I think it's time to get back to basics."

"I hope you're not implying," Roger says, a little defensively, "that my guys in the field don't care about relationships. As sales professionals, we're crystal clear that business is all about relationships."

"Roger, I know you have good people out there," Michael answers. "What I'm saying is that we've put so much pressure on them to sell that I believe it's changed the dynamic out there—the nature of the interaction that occurs between them and their customers. Also, we haven't been soliciting the Sales team's input in our product development process; we know many of our old products are getting stale. Plus, our marketing efforts have been weak. Overall, I think to some extent, we've failed our Sales team. It's time for a renewal. Our Sales folks hear what our customers think and we're not listening to them."

"I think it all comes back to communication," Alan adds. "The snapshot we did of the top 200 leaders indicates what others are saying, too: employees don't feel valued and appreciated and they don't feel we have an open and honest work environment. I think part of this has to do with not asking people for their ideas, for their input, in addition to not listening when they do offer suggestions. We have a lot of meetings around here, but I'm not sure that we've been listening in those meetings!"

"I agree," says Kim. "I can see now that we have issues concerning our direction, strategic planning and communication. I know that you're probably going to be shocked to hear me say this, but the work that we've begun on improving ourselves as leaders and beginning the process of improving this culture is as important as those other issues. We made a commitment to the Board to drive out another $50 million in expenses this year. Given that we've already downsized, and we've said we're not going to do any more of that, a lot of heavy lifting is still ahead of us. And, with the culture we currently have, as Alan has reminded us, the process improvement work will be 100 times more difficult to do—it may even be impossible. What I'm saying is that *we need to hear the voice of our employees, the people who operate these processes, to help us improve them. It has to be a top-down and bottom-up initiative.*"

Jen nods, "I couldn't agree with you more, Kim."

Michael turns to Brian. "I know we're getting close to the end of the day. Will we have an opportunity at some point to begin planning how we'll deal with some of these issues?"

"Well, Michael," Brian answers, "I've got some good news and some more good news. Yes, we'll have some time at the end of the day to talk about next steps regarding planning, and everything that you've talked about in the last forty-five minutes will fit into that planning work."

"So, what's the other good news?" David asks him.

"When it comes to facilitating that work, you have a highly qualified person in Jen," Brian answers. "She's had a lot of experience in creating and executing culture-change plans."

"Great!" Alan says.

"Michael," Kim says, with a slight tone of jealousy, "this is probably the best hiring decision you've made in some time."

"Thank you, Kim," Jen says.

Roger asks Kim whether she's being sarcastic. Kim answers sharply, "I meant what I said, Roger. Now stop trying to cause trouble!"

"Before we move on," Michael says, ignoring this last exchange, "I want to reiterate two of the things we learned from Brian today. First, each of us must make a commitment to being accountable as we continue leading this company. Second, we must use ourselves as instruments of change and think and behave like business owners. Let's make 'accountability' a cornerstone of Horton & Oliver's new culture."

Over the next few hours the team reviews the team survey results. The most important issues to be addressed pertain to a need for more:

- Openness,

- Honesty,

- Communication, and

- Value and appreciation felt by team members.

Based on these results and the previous work that had been done with regard to meeting ground rules, Brian facilitates the team through the process of creating ***behaviors that each team member commits to living on a daily basis to improve the effectiveness of the team's interactions, decisions, etc.—team norms of behavior.***

Next, working in pairs, each team member takes two minutes to share with other team members what they value about them and what they believe their teammates can do to add even more value to the company. After multiple rounds of this kind of sharing, Brian is moved by the palpable increase in positive energy as team members engage in their feedback conversations. He is pleased to see that there is no defensiveness. On the contrary, team members are following the practice of coming from a place of ***curiosity rather than judgment*** in their interactions. The activity is one of the highlights of the retreat. Team members note that they got more useful feedback in the thirty-minute activity than they had received in the past year!

Based on this feedback, each team member creates one ***personal commitment statement***, focusing on an area of ***personal behavior change that will have a positive impact on operating as a team and leading the company***. Team members commit to the following:

- Michael to listening more effectively.

- Jen to providing more positive than constructive feedback.

- Kim to approaching conversations from curiosity rather than judgment.

- Alan to becoming a more courageous communicator in executive team meetings—saying what he's thinking instead of holding back.

- Roger to communicating clearer performance expectations to his people.

- David to thinking and behaving more like an owner, particularly in providing feedback to members of the team when he sees them doing something positive and when he sees them doing something that needs to be corrected.

After those commitments are publicly shared, Brian asks the team to form two coaching trios that will meet on a weekly basis for the next three months. The two purposes of the coaching trios are to discuss the progress they're making with regard to their personal commitments and to solicit and receive feedback from their peers. Michael, Alan, and Kim form one coaching trio; Jen, Roger, and David form the other.

As the retreat draws to a close, Brian asks Jen to guide the team through the process of planning the next steps for Horton & Oliver's culture-change effort. She turns to Brian and says, "I'd like to use one of your models to guide this process: the 'Organization Alignment & Change Model.'" Brian nods his head in agreement.

After she talks through the model with the team, she revisits the input that was given during the accountability activity earlier in the day. "To recap what we discussed today, when we did the accountability/ownership activity, we said that we needed to focus on visioning, strategic planning, employee and customer communication, culture change, and employee engagement."

Organization Alignment & Change Model

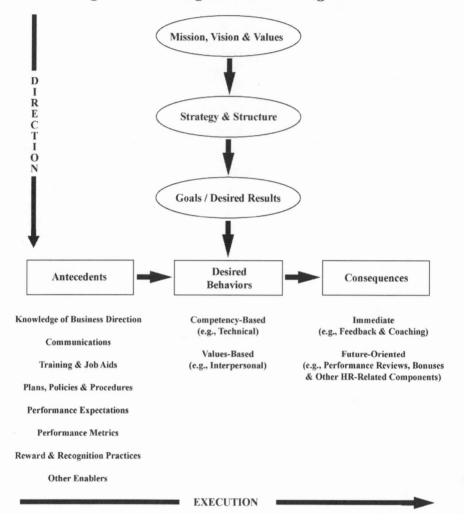

Organization Alignment & Change Model
Definitions

Mission: *What* we are in business to do.

Vision: *Who* we aspire to become as a company or organization.

Values: *What* guides how we conduct ourselves in the workplace and in the marketplace.

Strategy: *What* we do to win customers and differentiate ourselves from our competition; this includes our strategic and tactical plans.

Structure: *How* we organize and operate to achieve our Mission, Vision, and Strategy. This includes our organizational structure and our infrastructure (i.e., operating systems).

Goals/Desired Results: *What* we set as performance targets to direct and measure success.

Desired Behaviors: *How* we expect people to behave in order to achieve our Goals/Desired Results.

Antecedents: *What* prompts behavior and gets it going; 20% of the impact on human behavior comes from Antecedents. This percentage goes up when an Antecedent is paired with a Consequence.

Consequences: *What* a person experiences after s/he behaves that makes it more or less likely that they will behave that way again; 80% of the impact on human behavior comes from Consequences. Consequences become Antecedents of future behavior in the form of thoughts, etc. The most powerful consequences are immediate consequences such as feedback and coaching.

"As you can see, all of these components fit nicely in Brian's Organization Alignment & Change Model. To further flesh this out, one piece that we have not addressed is the need to revisit the values of the company. We need to determine if they are the right ones to lead us into the future, given the vision that we will create.

"Then we need to *behavioralize those values so people will know specifically what we expect of them in terms of their everyday behavior.* The values and associated behaviors that we create will become the *norms of behavior for the entire corporation; they will define our desired culture.*

"So, if we use the Organization Alignment & Change Model as our guide, our first order of business is to *revisit our mission, vision and values*—these are among the key elements that will define our new business direction.

"The second is to *create a strategy and structure—organizational structure and infrastructure (i.e., operating systems)*—that will move us in the desired direction. The third is to *identify performance goals or desired results* so that we can target and measure our success. The fourth step is to *identify the behaviors* that are needed to drive desired results. And these behaviors fall into two categories: *competency-based* or technical behaviors needed to do specific jobs, and then the *values-based* behaviors we talked about earlier.

"Fifth, we need to identify the appropriate antecedents that will support getting the desired behaviors going across the company. For our antecedents, we need to plan in *three major areas: communication, education, and measurement.* Our sixth action involves *focusing on consequences.* This is where we have to *align all of the HR Systems* in the company. This alignment will involve creating internal consistency between our performance management, compensation, hiring, employee orientation, and succession planning systems—all of them—and the desired behaviors and results we're trying to achieve as a company. Finally, we need to determine how we will create a coaching- and feedback-rich culture. *When it comes to shaping desired behavior, immediate consequences, such as feedback and coaching, are the most powerful.* "

"This makes a lot of sense," says Kim as she looks at Brian.

"Thank you," Brian says quietly.

Jen continues, "If we're in agreement that these are the logical next steps, the question becomes, 'How should we approach this work?'"

"I think what needs to be done is clear, we just need the time to do it." David says. He continues, "We all have a tremendous amount of desire to get this work done. Am I right?"

"Absolutely," Kim says as the rest of the team nods their heads.

"We have a lot going on," says Michael, "but I would suggest that we need to clear the decks two weeks from Friday and spend all day Friday and all day Saturday creating our culture-change plan."

"I'm sure I can have the remaining company culture results for you by then," Brian offers.

"I hate to give up a Saturday with my family," Alan says, "but if I'm thinking like an owner, this is a must-do."

"I agree with you completely, Alan," Jen says. "You've noticed that I reserve weekends for family time. May I explain why I feel so strongly about this?" The team members nod—they're interested in hearing more. "I believe each of us needs to balance home and work if we expect to be at our best in either place. For me, it comes down to giving full attention to work while I'm at the office. If I am working as efficiently and effectively as I can at Horton & Oliver, I believe weekend work can be kept to a minimum. Now, all of that being said, Alan is right. This planning has to take priority right now."

When Michael looks around the room seeking input, he finds unanimous agreement. "In preparation for the meeting," Jen says, "I want to ask each person to review our current mission and vision statements, our current values, and our existing strategic plan."

Alan offers to send each team member a copy of the current communication and HR plans.

"I've been doing some work on our performance goals," Kim suggests. "I'll send copies to the team."

"Good work. It sounds like we have a plan," Michael says.

Brian closes the meeting by giving each member an opportunity to talk about how they're feeling at the end of the two days and to share words of appreciation for one another. He reminds them of how important it is to celebrate steps, even small ones, in the change process. It's clear from listening to the team that they're on a high and there is a new sense of hope and optimism about the future of Horton & Oliver and their ability to lead the company where it needs to go.

As people get up to leave, there are warm handshakes and smiles, even some hugs. As Brian waves goodbye, he says, "Remember accountability—think and behave like owners!"

"Thank you, Brian," they each answer.

The days following the retreat brought about continued self-reflection, sharing, learning, and change. At dinner Saturday night, Kim asks her significant other whether he sees her as judgmental or confrontational. Bill laughs. "Are you being serious?"

"No, Bill, I'm joking," she says dryly. She catches herself instantly, flashing on that slide from the retreat: Stimulus → Response <u>OR</u> Stimulus → Pause and Choose → Response. "There I go again," she thinks to herself, "back on autopilot. Damn, this is hard!"

Before Bill can answer, Kim apologizes. "I didn't mean to be sarcastic. I am being sincere and I really do want to know what you think. I care about our relationship. I'm afraid that I've been far too judgmental of you."

Bill's smile turns to a look of concern. "You really are being serious, aren't you? Wow. I don't know what to say."

"Just tell me the truth," Kim answers.

Bill responds, "We've been together for three years now. Over those three years, I've thought you were finished with me at least a couple of dozen times. I often wonder whether I can ever do anything right in your eyes. If I weren't so crazy about you, I would have been out of here a long time ago."

Kim's eyes begin to well up and she can't hold back the tears. Bill asks, "What's wrong? What did I do?"

"Bill, it isn't you, it's me," Kim says quietly. "I'm really disappointed in myself. My mentors in the business world did a really good job of toughening me up so I could break through the glass ceiling. The only problem is I've become a real bitch in the process."

Bill offers his handkerchief. Kim accepts and whispers her thanks.

"I never cry," she says, shaking her head. "I must be losing my mind."

"What's going on, Kim?"

Kim describes the past week's retreat and the feedback she received. She tells him about the insights she gained about her *behavior and its impact*.

"Don't be so tough on yourself." Bill says. "I don't know anyone who's perfect."

"Bill, I truly want to change. *At work I made a commitment to come from a place of curiosity instead of judgment. I want to do the same in my personal life*. I want to do the same with you."

"How can I help?"

"Let me know when I'm slipping. This won't be easy for me. It's almost like an addiction."

"Kim, I don't want to sound patronizing, but I'm happy for you. I'm really impressed."

"Thanks."

"While we're on the subject, I know I make mistakes too. Kim, let me have it. What can I do to make our relationship better?"

She starts laughing through the tears. "I didn't believe Brian when he told us ***this work is 24/7***, but, here we are." To herself, Kim adds, "So, this is what it takes!"

Your Turn: Be a *Change Agent*

1. Consider your behavior and its impact with respect to each of these leadership principles:

Being Accountable
My behavior:

Its impact:

Being Authentic
My behavior:

Its impact:

Respecting and Leveraging Separate Realities
My behavior:

Its impact:

Using Curiosity Instead of Judgment
My behavior:

Its impact:

Providing and Soliciting Feedback
My behavior:

Its impact:

Being In the Moment
My behavior:

Its impact:

Celebrating Progress
My behavior:

Its impact:

2. Think about your personal behavior. Are there changes you could make that would have a positive impact on your performance? Which single behavior would you change to have the greatest impact? Are you willing to make a personal commitment now to change that behavior?

3. Is there a colleague of yours whom you can ask for support in making the behavioral change identified in Question 2? Are you willing to ask that colleague to give you regular feedback? If you are, please do so within the next week!

4. How would your company or organization benefit from a retreat like the one the Horton & Oliver team experienced? Why?

Culture change begins with personal change.

CHAPTER 6

▼

LOOKING IN THE MIRROR

"Self-knowledge is the beginning of self-improvement."
—Spanish proverb

Week Five

Maybe he has a career at Horton & Oliver after all, David tells himself. For the past year or so, he'd had serious doubts. His friends and colleagues had been surprised when he'd signed on at H&O in the first place. They'd helped him celebrate a series of impressive victories that had earned him high standing in the legal community. What his friends hadn't realized was the toll that those victories had taken on David personally. He was exhausted and ready to leave courtroom battles behind—at least for awhile.

The offer from Horton & Oliver was made more interesting when David met Michael and Richard (H&O's former COO). Both seemed to be men of principle and integrity. David found their sense of loyalty and honor refreshing. H&O promised the type of workplace for which he'd been looking. Watching Richard leave had dealt a blow to David's morale.

The work the executive team is doing now, especially the retreat last week, feels to David like a return to living the company's values. He is certain others on the team share his hope that taking this path to restoring H&O's focus on customers and employees will bolster not only the company's performance, but also the team's sense of worth. He is confident that Michael is committed to staying the course.

Michael never celebrates his birthday at the office, but his assistant enters the Monday morning meeting with Edward behind her. Edward is carrying a cake, the candles are lit and everyone begins singing "Happy Birthday." "Since we don't have pastries and fruit, I thought you should have a cake," Ruth tells Michael. As she brings paper plates and plastic forks to the table, she turns to the team and says, "If I may share something…"

Michael says, "Of course, Ruth, by all means."

"You know I'm not shy, and I like to share good news—especially now that we finally have some." Ruth catches herself. "I'm sorry. That didn't come out exactly the way I meant it."

"Please, go on," Michael encourages her.

"I have to say, I am hearing so many good things on this floor and throughout the building about the positive changes that are starting to take place at Horton & Oliver. It may have seemed like a small thing to do, but closing the executive dining room and having lunch with the employees has made a very favorable impression. I don't think people knew what to make of it at first—some even wondered what you all were up to. I think people are starting to believe now that the old Horton & Oliver family feeling is coming back. You know, Mr. Horton used to eat his lunch every day in the cafeteria. He thought it was part of what made us a family."

"I came in to hear about your retreat," Edward says. "But after hearing what Ruth just had to say, it sounds like things are on the right track. Michael, you and I can catch up later to discuss the specifics." Edward raises his coffee cup in salute and offers a toast to Michael on his birthday. Then he turns to the team and says, "Keep up the good work. Now cut that cake, Michael. I'll take mine to go."

The team soon gets down to business. At the end of the meeting, Michael reminds the team, "Please complete the pre-reading we discussed at last week's retreat. As you know, Jen will be facilitating our planning meeting. Jen, is there anything you'd like to add?"

"Yes. Please add one thing to your reading list—Brian's culture audit. Beyond that, I just have a reminder. *We need to focus on continuing to improve our individual and team behaviors*. In the spirit of creating a *feedback-rich culture*, let's put our emphasis on *celebrating desired behavior when we observe it and correcting undesired behavior—including our own.* Remember what Brian told us: *80% of the impact on human behavior comes from consequences, because consequences shape our beliefs which, in turn, drive our behaviors.*" Jen continues, "When people hear the word 'consequences' they almost always think of something negative; but, when it comes to shaping new behaviors or motivating people, delivering positive consequences is a vital part of the process. What we learned from Brian is that *the average employee, over time, needs to hear four times as many positive pieces of feedback as constructive pieces to stay motivated and to give discretionary effort.* Many of the executives I've worked with deliver far more criticism and constructive feedback than positive feedback. So, what's the message?"

Alan jumps in. "We need to use more positive reinforcement to shape desired behavior!"

"I could not have said it any better, Alan," Jen tells him.

"Now I've got another thing to worry about," Roger says, barely hiding his frustration. "Please tell me all of this is going to settle down soon."

Kim answers him. "It's really pretty simple, Roger. Think of the Golden Rule. 'Treat others the way you want to be treated.'

"Actually," Kim adds, "a better approach is, '*Treat people the way they want to be treated.*'" As they wrap things up, Jen reminds the coaching teams that they have less than ten days to have their first coaching meeting prior to the planning session.

"Before we adjourn," Michael says, "I'd like to ask a favor of Jen." She nods her consent. "Jen, we're trying to make some big, difficult changes around here," he continues. "As we move ahead, I'd like to ask you to help keep us all honest, to help us hold to our personal commitments as a team."

"I'm comfortable with that," Jen says. "But honestly, we all need to make that commitment to one another." The team agrees. Almost involuntarily, however, Roger sighs deeply and audibly. Michael stops and glances his way and leaves the room.

As the week goes on, it is clear that the improvements are continuing at Horton & Oliver. Not only are executive staff meetings more focused and productive, but the meetings at the next level down are also improving. The meeting ground rules are observed. Customers and their needs are frequently the focus, and, when they aren't, the indirect impact on the customer is clear. Leaders have begun consistently asking about "customer benefit and impact" when in discussion with their staffs. Jen is pleased to note that, in her division and throughout the company, people are coming to meetings more prepared and are doing a better job of facilitating timely decision making.

The biggest change is between the executive team and their direct reports. Members of the executive team are asking for input; there is a greater sense of collaboration, at least at the top two levels of the corporation. The senior team is focused on delivering more positive reinforcement as it pertains to living the meeting rules and becoming more customer-focused. Employees and customers are continuing to say it feels different at H&O. They feel a more positive energy at the top of the company.

Kim creates a process-improvement strategy to drive out waste. It is designed to involve employees from every level. Named by a member of her staff, it is called the "Waste-Not Challenge."

Michael decides he and Roger should visit with H&O's top 25 customers. He asks Roger to set up these meetings.

Week Six

Jen, Roger, and David agree that their coaching trio will schedule a meeting each Monday from 5:00-6:00 p.m. as a standing meeting. Their first meeting is on the Monday just before the planning session.

Everyone arrives at David's office on time. David closes the door and turns to Jen. "Jen, you've been through this before. Would you mind facilitating our coaching meeting?"

"Really," says Roger, "I don't have a clue what we should be doing here."

Jen answers, "I'd be delighted to."

She pulls out her journal and says, "Why not begin by restating what each of us committed to improving at the retreat? My personal commitment was to deliver more positive feedback than constructive feedback. David, I wrote down that you are focusing on coming from a place of accountability, behaving more like an owner, with a particular focus on providing positive and constructive feedback to team members. Roger, for you I have that you were going to work on providing clearer performance expectations to your direct reports. At the retreat, we talked about each of us keeping a personal journal where we would document successes and opportunities for improvement. Although it was not explicitly stated, the intention is that we would focus on living all of the team behavior norms in addition to focusing on the one personal area where we need the most improvement."

"That's what has me concerned, Jen," says Roger. "I'm finding myself being so worried about what I do and how I do it that I've lost what makes me successful as a sales person, that's my spontaneity, saying what comes to mind in the moment."

"Roger, are you saying that you're thinking so much about your behavior that it's getting in the way of your spontaneity?" David asks.

"That's exactly what I'm saying."

"That's not unusual, Roger," Jen tells him. ***"Whenever we are learning something new or trying to implement change, at first it requires a level of concentration that may feel unnatural, but eventually it will become second nature.*** It's no different than when you first learned to ride a bike. At first, you had to be so deliberate in every movement, every action. With time, though, it all became second nature to you.

"Roger, since you've gotten the ball rolling, tell us what kind of progress you've made this week in terms of living the team norms and improving the clarity of performance expectations."

"Well, I gotta tell you up front, I'm not keeping a journal. I started to, but one of my guys made a crack about 'Dear Diary!'"

"And you let that get in the way of doing it?" David asks.

"Not exactly," Roger tells him. "I've got such a good memory that I don't think I really need to keep a diary, I mean a journal."

"So, we've got about forty-five minutes left," Jen says. "That leaves fifteen minutes for each of us to talk about progress we've made and difficulties we've faced, and get feedback from our coaching mates."

Roger starts off. "We're doing great. In the last week, I've had two performance discussions. They went really well. I've got more to do next week. I'm sure they'll be fine."

"Roger, you said you wanted to work on providing more clarity as it pertains to providing performance expectations," Jen reminds him. "Can you tell us specifically how you did this differently over the past week?"

"You know. I was clear! I told them what they needed to do."

David steps in. "I think what Jen's trying to get at is what made these discussions different from discussions you've had in the past. What did you do differently, Roger?"

"This is starting to feel like an inquisition," Roger says quickly. "Take my word for it. It went better."

David decides to back off. Jen turns to him. "David, how was your week?"

"Well, I was looking for a way to measure my progress, so I put together a chart," he says. "I'm keeping track of the number of opportunities I have each day to give feedback and how many of those opportunities I seize and use to deliver it."

"That's great," Jen tells him. "Are you keeping track of the people to whom you're providing feedback?"

"My system is kind of elementary right now, but I'm writing the initials of the people in my planner. Right now, I'm just trying to become more aware of the frequency with which I'm giving feedback."

"That's a great first step," Jen says.

"I never dreamed that I had so many opportunities," David continues. "I counted up the opportunities of the past week and came up with over sixty. So far, I've delivered nineteen pieces of positive feedback and seven pieces of constructive feedback."

Roger seems distracted. He's checking his Palm Pilot, looking out the window, and reading the cover of the magazine David keeps on his coffee table.

"If I may pass on one golden nugget that I learned from Brian, it's **to think of constructive feedback as an opportunity to deliver future positive feedback,**" Jen says.

Roger lifts his head up: "Huh?"

"Every time I give a person a piece of constructive feedback, my job is to catch them taking a positive step toward the target behavior and to recognize that step using positive feedback."

"You mean we shouldn't just provide constructive feedback and walk away," David says, nodding. "We should catch people making incremental improvements and reward them with positive feedback."

"Exactly!" responds Jen.

"I get it," David says. "So, how have you been doing, Jen?"

"Well, I'm still a newbie and I'm still getting to know my direct reports. I've been journaling about the occasions when I've given feedback. So far, I'm doing a pretty good job of maintaining that four-to-one ratio Brian spoke about. The thing that's really exciting to me is the impact that it's having. I'm having a much easier time getting to know these folks because I'm taking time to celebrate the good work they do. When I have constructive feedback to offer, it feels as though they are more receptive. Beyond that, I've been amazed at the number of people who have asked what more they can do to help. That's what I call discretionary effort!"

Jen takes a moment to consider. "I've also been striving to achieve the four-to-one ratio with members of our team. I won't share all of the positives that I've delivered, but I would like to tell you about the impact of some constructive feedback I gave to Michael. By the way, he gave me permission to share this with members of our team."

Roger has returned to the conversation on hearing Michael's name.

"Michael was complaining to me about the lack of progress that he was seeing in one of our divisions—I won't say which one. So, what I did was ask him what more he could do about it."

"You mean you were challenging the old man?" Roger asks.

"That's not quite how I'd put it. I'd ask him to look through the lens of accountability and ask himself, 'What more can I do in this situation to make a difference?' The neat thing is that, within thirty seconds, he came up with a solution that he planned to implement. This may seem like a very small thing, but I find that too often people complain about others without taking action. Trust me, if you owned this company, you would not hesitate to do what needed to be done to rectify a situation. *In this situation, accountability means providing upward feedback.*"

"That's a great example, Jen," David says. "I agree with you about the complaining thing. I can see how this thing called accountability can really make a difference. It's already making a difference in terms of the amount of feedback I'm providing. I keep asking myself, what would I do if I owned this company? Clearly, I would be intervening more often than I did in the past. After hearing what you did, I might feel more comfortable providing constructive feedback to Michael."

Roger wonders aloud, "I'm not ready to go there. By the way, are we done yet?"

"Well we still have ten minutes left," David answers. He turns to Jen, "Is there anything else we should talk about?"

"In the spirit of accountability, Roger, I need to go back to our discussion at the beginning of this meeting," she says. "My observation was that you became a bit defensive when David asked you to speak in specific terms about what you've done differently over the past week regarding performance expectations. I heard you say this felt like an inquisition. If we're going to be successful, we're going to need to be able to talk to each other about how we're doing and ask for help if we need it. We also need to be open to receiving feedback in order to create a feedback-rich culture at H&O. This is mandatory."

"Yeah, I got defensive," Roger admits. "I'm just not as skilled in this area as you guys are. I'll get better."

"Roger, is there anything I can do to support you?" Jen asks. "I know making these personal changes is not easy, but remember, it's about progress, not perfection. Let's celebrate baby steps."

"I'm sorry I got defensive," Roger says to David. "You were right to ask me to be more specific. Damn. Maybe I need to keep a journal after all."

David smiles and says, "That's all right, buddy."

"In the couple of minutes we have left," Jen says, "let's talk about what went well in this meeting and what we need to do differently next time to be even more effective. We call this type of meeting evaluation a *Plus-Delta activity. The 'Plus' is obvious: what did we do well? The 'Delta' is the Greek symbol for change: what can we change to be even more effective next time?*"

Your Turn: Be a *Change Agent*

1. At the very end of the chapter, Jen suggested conducting a "Plus-Delta" activity to assess the meeting. What would say were the "Pluses" or positive elements of the meeting? What would you say were the "Deltas" or areas for improvement?

2. What are your beliefs about delivering and receiving feedback? Are your beliefs about delivering or receiving feedback different if the feedback is positive or if it is constructive?

3. How often do you provide positive and constructive feedback to the people who work for you? How about to the person/people for whom you work? How about to your peers? If there is a difference in your responses, why do you think that is the case?

4. How often do you receive feedback, positive or constructive, from those for whom you work, those you work with and those who work for you? How do you feel about the feedback you receive from these different groups of people?

5. If you chose to seek a coaching relationship with a colleague at the end of Chapter 5, what can you do to ensure that relationship is successful?

The only person I can truly change is myself.

CHAPTER 7

▼

CREATING A PLAN OF ACTION

"Before everything else, getting ready is the secret of success."
—*Henry Ford*

Week Six, Friday

When the Friday of the two-day planning session arrives, the team is ready to get down to work. Early on, Jen shows the group one of Brian's slides, depicting a set of scales, holding teamwork in one dish and taskwork in the other. She explains that the term "taskwork" refers to the "what"—the tasks they'll undertake in the session. "We'll work on mission, vision, values, creating a plan to address strategy, structure, goals/desired results, the behaviors to produce those results, the antecedents of communication, education and measurement, and the consequences of feedback and coaching and aligning our HR Systems."

As they are discussing the model, Jen puts up another slide, identical to the Organization Alignment & Change Model slide used at the retreat, except that the word CULTURE covers the bottom of the page. "The culture of the organization (that is, learned behavior) is shaped by antecedents and consequences," she says. "The desired culture has to be aligned with the organization's mission, vision, and values."

Organization Alignment & Change Model

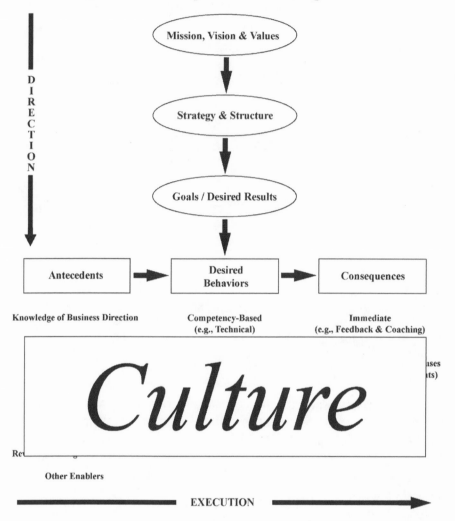

Referring back to the scale slide, on the teamwork side, Jen tells them they will focus on the "how"—living their team norms of behavior in addition to their personal commitments as they proceed through the day. She says, "Brian calls this approach *'Action Learning'—working on tasks while practicing new team behaviors.*"

"In other words," she tells the group, "we'll accomplish the business tasks while living the desired behaviors that we've identified at the individual and team levels."

As she talks about teamwork, Jen hangs a poster on the wall. It lists the norms of behavior the team agreed upon at the retreat; these norms include the team's meeting ground rules. She tells them she finds it helpful to have as a reminder.

"I hope you don't mind that I've borrowed your idea, Kim," she adds. Kim shakes her head and smiles, obviously pleased. "In fact," says Jen, "you inspired me to try something else. Here is a gift for each of you." Jen hands out a laminated, pocket-size card to each team member. On one side, the norms of behavior are listed. On the other are the personal commitments each person made at the retreat. Once everyone has a card to keep, Jen walks them through the Organization Alignment & Change Model again. "Today, our objective is to have a serious discussion about our mission, vision, and values. We'll also create a 'culture-change plan' to address the other key components of this model.

"In the spirit of continuous improvement, every two hours or so, I'll ask the team to stop and break into our coaching trios. Then we'll use the ***ARC Learning Methodology: Awareness, Reflection, and Choice***, to reflect on the behavior we've exhibited and to give each other feedback. Last, we'll do some personal journaling to document what each of us wants to continue doing, stop doing, and start doing based on that feedback."

The team members spend the first day looking at their mission, vision, and values. Although they find there are few wording changes to be made to the mission, the vision changes dramatically. Horton & Oliver has been steadily losing market share. After years as the industry leader, the company has dropped to number three in the market. The old vision called for Horton & Oliver to be the "most respected supplier in their industry." The team's new vision for H&O states, among other things, that it will regain market share and return to the number one spot. Their goal is to achieve that in the next five years!

Before they delve into values, the group discusses the culture audit of the entire company. The results closely parallel those for H&O's top 200 leaders, with one exception. Two more statements are added to those that received the worst scores. These two new entries to the survey's red or "danger zone" reflect that people are not optimistic about H&O's future and that they don't feel empowered to be creative and take risks. The report shows results by functional area and a composite for the entire company. The worst results reported are in the Sales department. One more statement shows up in the danger zone in Sales only: "People are not held accountable for achieving results."

The team discusses the implications of the audit and decides to alter the values and adopt some new ones. They discuss the values that they hold deeply as a team and that would guide Horton & Oliver toward achieving their newly defined vision.

The new list of Horton & Oliver's values is:

I CARE:
Integrity
Customer-Focused
Accountability
Respect
Employees First

As the team moves on to develop its culture-change plan, they revisit the Organization Alignment & Change Model Jen presented earlier. They develop a list of to-do items:

DIRECTION –

Align the strategy, structure, and goals/desired results with the new vision.

DESIRED BEHAVIORS –

Use employee focus groups to behavioralize Horton & Oliver's five newly identified values.

ANTECEDENTS –

1. Create a comprehensive communication plan that communicates the direction and desired culture of H&O and solicits feedback from employees.

2. Create an education plan that focuses on cascading a proven methodology that will:

    a. Unfreeze old beliefs,

    b. Shape new beliefs and behavioral habits aligned with H&O's values and associated behaviors,

    c. Teach core leadership principles and skills, such as "be in the moment," "accountability," and "feedback and coaching" that will guide the shaping of H&O's new culture, and

    d.   Create a "common language" within the company and a "shared reality" among all employees regarding the direction of H&O and the values/behaviors that are necessary to succeed.

3.   Create a measurement plan to track progress by focusing on both behaviors and results.

CONSEQUENCES –

1.   Revamp the Performance Management System to mandate formal bi-monthly feedback and coaching sessions for all employees. Incorporate an online 360-Degree Feedback Survey into the annual performance review and development process so each management employee can receive feedback on how well they are living H&O's values, and so they can create personal development plans to make improvements.

2.   Align all HR Systems with the values and behaviors that will produce desired results.

By the end of day two of the planning session, the team has created a Gantt Chart outlining all of the activities needed to implement the culture-change plan. The Gantt Chart includes the work to be done and the start and end dates for each task. The chart they developed will keep them focused on the to-do list. It's a very productive day and each person has several opportunities to contribute and provide feedback.

As the planning session draws to a close, Jen prepares to turn things back over to Michael. First, she leads the team in a Plus-Delta meeting evaluation similar to the one she facilitated with her coaching trio. The pluses far outnumber the deltas. Throughout the planning session, team members lived the norms they had established. Team members congratulate Michael for listening to them closely. Alan tells him, "I guess I had kind of gotten used to the old behavioral patterns you and I had fallen into, Michael. Now I really appreciate it when you are genuinely listening to my suggestions and considering my ideas!"

David tells Kim that he knows she had to bite her tongue occasionally and that she may have been impatient with his proposals at times, but "I feel as though you were sincerely interested in understanding my point of view. Thank you, Kim."

"Thank you, David," Kim answers.

It's clear that some team members are making significant progress in fulfilling their personal commitments. "Congratulations," Jen says. "Remember, we've only been working on this for a little more than a month. We've already accomplished quite a lot. I'm confident we will continue to change things at Horton & Oliver for the better."

Then Michael stands up to close the meeting. There is a level of energy in his voice that the team hasn't heard in some time (in fact, some of them had never heard him like this)—and this is after two exhausting days of work. He thanks the team for their hard work and thanks Jen for her expert facilitation. "If you had told me a month ago," Michael says, "that we would have a detailed plan in place to turn this company around, I would never have thought it possible. This is so important to Horton & Oliver that, from now on, we'll begin every Monday morning meeting on the topic of culture change and include an update on progress with our plan.

"Remember, though, the plan is just one component of this process of transforming Horton & Oliver and its culture. I'm convinced it all comes down to our behavior. The execution of this plan, plus the Waste-Not Challenge Kim is managing, depends upon our behavior. The bottom line is it's about *living our values. Our values must guide everything we do at H&O.* We will not tolerate anything less from ourselves or from anyone associated with our company. Our future depends on it."

He turns to Alan. "With you as our HR and communication guru, I can't wait to hit the ground running in the next two weeks and begin conducting our first town hall meetings to share our new vision and values. I know that we don't have all the answers yet, but I feel it's long overdue that I am out there talking with and, more importantly, listening to our folks!"

Michael concludes by addressing the team, looking at each one in turn. "I want to meet with each of you individually over the next week to talk about the audit results in your area and my expectations for improvement over the next year. I have contracted with Brian to provide executive coaching, starting with me. I'll clarify with each of you how that will work for you."

Once the meeting is over, a few team members stay to chat and some leave. The mood is one of satisfaction. As she heads home, Jen realizes that this is becoming a very different team from the one she first met. She realizes she is beginning to feel at home.

Your Turn: Be a *Change Agent*

1. How relevant are your company's or organization's values to the day-to-day operations of the company or organization?

2. If your company or organization does not have a defined set of values, what does your leadership team believe are the principles that guide—or should guide—your company or organization? In establishing your values, consider those that you share as a leadership team that need to be shared by the entire company or organization.

3. What behaviors are your Performance Management System and other HR Systems reinforcing today? Are these behaviors consistent with your company's or organization's values?

4. If your HR Systems are not aligned with your company's or organization's values, what is the impact? What can be done to align these systems with the values and desired behaviors?

5. Take a look at the Organization Alignment & Change Model on page 62. Which of the components in the model (if any) need to be strengthened in your company or organization? What plan would you create for accomplishing this?

You can only create what you can define.

PART III

▼

The Journey Continues

CHAPTER 8

▼

MAKING COURAGEOUS DECISIONS

"Wherever you see a successful business, someone once made a courageous decision."
—*Peter Drucker*

Week Six, Saturday

Roger leaves the planning session certain that he has a very different feeling about it than his peers. To him, it's all pointless, "touchy-feely" talk. If they'd just stop creating new rules and let his Sales guys do their job, the company would be much better off. Now, it seems like Michael is expecting some kind of miracle from Sales. Doesn't he know the economy is only just starting to improve?

When he arrives home, Roger grabs a cold beer and flips open his cell phone to call one of his best friends.

Todd is a successful head hunter. Like Roger, he can be a smooth talker and thinks of himself as a people person. After some small talk, Roger begins to vent.

"You know I've been saying that H&O is in trouble," he says. "Remember the old saying about arranging the deck chairs on the *Titanic*? It's even worse than that. The ship is sinking and we're taking 'charm' classes! We've hired a consultant so we can learn to work better with one another. It's a bunch of bullshit! To make matters worse, all of my peers are drinking the Kool-Aid and liking it. Even Kim! I thought she was an ally. I'm convinced that all this crap is only going to make H&O sink faster."

Todd listens patiently and is not surprised when Roger asks him to quietly put his name out on the street. Roger is still exasperated when they hang up. "I don't know how much longer I can put up with this," he says.

Week Seven, Monday

After the Monday morning executive team meeting, Michael asks Alan to stay behind for a moment. He also asks Roger for time to meet. They arrange to meet later in the day to talk about the culture audit results in the Sales area.

Once Roger has left, Michael turns to Alan. "As we learned the other day, the department that scored the worst on the culture audit is Sales. Do you have any insights that would help me better understand what's been going on there?"

"I can tell you that I've been concerned about the high turnover in Sales," Alan tells him. "I've also been hearing grumbling about an 'old boy network.'"

Michael pauses to think. "We conduct exit interviews, don't we?"

"Of course," Alan answers. "We send a copy to the supervisor, one to the appropriate executive, and we keep the original in our files. If you'd like, I'll pull together some of the documentation."

"I'd appreciate it if you'd have someone get that to me this morning," Michael says.

When they meet that afternoon in his office, Michael begins the discussion by asking Roger how he feels about the changes taking place at H&O. Roger worries for an instant—how could Michael know I was talking to Todd—then he refocuses. Deciding to tell Michael what he wants to hear, Roger speaks glowingly of the retreat and subsequent planning session, careful to use the terminology he has heard from Brian and Jen. He is confident that Michael believes his sincerity.

"I'm delighted to hear this," Michael says. "That should make it easier to address the issues that were unearthed by the culture audit. I was struck by the fact that, in Sales, one of the areas that appears in the danger zone is people are not being held accountable for results. I'm also concerned about the high turnover rate among our Sales staff."

"I can understand why you'd be concerned," Roger says. "But what you may not realize is that Sales divisions everywhere are plagued with high turnover."

Michael hears Roger's condescension. Not only is he aware of the trend Roger describes, but he also knows that the turnover at H&O is far greater than the norm. He decides to let it go.

"Do you receive a copy of the exit interviews when Sales employees leave Horton & Oliver?" Michael asks.

"I think so. But where are we going with this, Michael?"

"Does that mean you read them?"

"C'mon, Michael," Roger shoots back. "I don't have time to read every piece of paper that hits my in-box."

Michael's face reddens. He pauses, takes a deep breath and looks directly at Roger. "I did take time today to read fifteen exit interviews conducted in the last four months alone. The thing that most concerns me is that the same themes emerged again and again: 'New ideas are dismissed out of hand.' People are told 'we don't do things that way around here,' 'if it's not broken, don't fix it' or 'we've tried that before, it didn't work.' On top of that, people complained that an 'old boy network is alive and well at H&O,' talking about favoritism and people being allowed to 'slide' based on how well they had performed in the past. Roger, we have to earn our reputation every day here. No one can rest on his or her laurels."

Roger is clearly angry. "Wait just a minute, Michael! It wasn't that long ago that you were telling everyone that H&O had let down the Sales team. Now you're pointing the blame at Sales. It sounds like you're talking out of both sides of your mouth!"

"Maybe we should have this conversation later," Michael says. "I remember what Brian said about moods, that *a low mood can be reflected in our behavior.* I'm afraid we may say something...excuse me, I'm afraid I may say something that I'll regret later. In keeping with our values, I want to make sure that this conversation remains respectful."

Raising his voice, Roger says: "Forget all that crap about feelings and moods, and all that values stuff! Don't you see what's happening here, Michael? You're letting this Jen woman and her buddy Brian lead you around by the nose!"

Michael rises to his feet. His voice is calm. "Really, Roger, I think we should continue this conversation later."

Roger jumps up from his chair, points his finger at Michael and says, "No! Let's finish this now."

"Okay, Roger. What is it you want to say?"

"I'm not going to become the scapegoat for all the problems that are going on here at H&O!" Roger screams. "First you blamed Richard and now you're blaming me!" Roger points his finger at Michael again. "Maybe you should be the one who's looking in the mirror!"

Trying to remain calm, Michael says to Roger, "Are you finished?"

"No," Roger answers loudly. "I'm just getting started!"

"Actually, Roger, you are finished. You're fired!"

With that, Michael picks up the phone, dials Ruth's extension and asks her to have security come to his office immediately. He turns to Roger and says: "I'm sorry it had to come to this. I'd like you to pack up your personal belongings and leave the building as soon as possible. Security will make sure everything goes smoothly."

Roger turns away from Michael, kicks a chair in front of Michael's desk and leaves the room. When he reaches the hallway, he meets two security guards who escort him to his office.

The loud voices have been creating a stir on the executive floor. When Roger finally walks out with his boxes, he is still fuming. "You'd better get out of here while you still can," he tells anyone who'll listen. "The old man has completely lost it!"

Responding to a request from Michael, Alan debriefs the CEO to ensure that the proper exit procedures are being followed. Michael also asks Alan to assemble the executive team for an urgent meeting at 5:30 p.m. that afternoon.

Michael's next call is to Brian.

From the tone of his voice, it is clear to Brian that Michael is upset about something. Brian listens as Michael describes the confrontation in detail from his own perspective. "From the way you describe it, it sounds as though your treatment of Roger was consistent with H&O's values," he tells Michael. "I'm sensing that there is something else bothering you."

"Yes there is. I can't let go of something Roger said," Michael answers. "He accused me of blaming H&O's problems on our former COO, Richard, and now on him. He doesn't know I fought to save Richard's job. Roger told me that I need to look in the mirror and stop blaming others. Maybe there's a hint of truth in that."

"Say more about that, Michael."

"I have the ultimate accountability for what happens at H&O. If someone's not doing his or her job properly, at the executive level, it's my job to coach him or her. I feel as though I failed Richard and now Roger. Maybe I'm the one who should be fired."

"Michael, what you've just shared is a powerful insight that you've gained about yourself," Brian replies. ***What's important now is not to dwell on the past, but to learn from it and make different choices going forward.*** The choices you've made over the past several weeks have been good ones. You've put H&O on a path to recovery. I would ask you to consider that perhaps it was time for Roger to go."

"Thank you, Brian," Michael says. "This has been helpful."

When the executive team gathers that evening, the air is solemn. "I guess you've heard by now that I chose to let Roger go," Michael tells them. "I don't feel comfortable sharing the details. Let's just say that we had a difference of opinion about the future direction of H&O. I'm disappointed that this had to happen, but I'm confident that the people sitting around this table will be able to continue the journey we've started together.

"I've made some immediate decisions that I'd like to share with you regarding the Sales organization. In the interim period, as Alan is contacting a search firm to begin the process of hiring a new Sales executive, I will be dividing my time between acting as CEO and running the Sales organization. Obviously, I will need your help to make this work effectively."

He turns to Alan. "I'd like your thoughts on how best to notify the Sales organization about the changes we are making.

"This next item is in your area, too, Alan," Michael continues. "Regarding the town hall meetings we talked about conducting as part of the culture-change plan, I want to meet with the top 200 leaders in the next two weeks to talk about our new vision and values. Following that, I want to conduct a town hall meeting with the Sales organization. The remaining town hall meetings will need to follow those two."

"Now," Michael says. "What questions do you have?"

After a somber moment, David speaks up. "I don't have a question. I have a comment. I feel badly that Roger is not with us anymore, but I'm more concerned about how you're doing, Michael." The others nod.

"Today has been a rough day," Michael answers. "I feel badly about Roger, but I feel it was the right decision to make."

"Roger's been one of my best friends in this company," Kim offers. "But I can tell you he was having difficulty with our new direction—especially our work around culture change. I'm not sure he ever would have been fully on board."

"When it comes to changing the culture of this company," Alan adds, **"We'll only be as strong as our weakest link.** I think you'll find in the long run that doing this will make us stronger."

Jen has been silent until now. "I agree with what others have said. My question is how can we best support you now?"

Michael looks to the team and says: "I appreciate the support you've demonstrated in this meeting. Thank you for that. No one said change was going to be easy, particularly when it comes to changing yourself. If I've learned anything over the past month—and it was reinforced today—it's that if this culture is going to change, I have to lead the way and model the behaviors I expect others to adopt. My commitment is to be that role model. What I need from you is for you to be role models, too!"

Jen looks around the table to her colleagues before speaking up. "Michael, you have my commitment. I suspect you have it from each of us." The others nod in agreement. "I'd like to add that it is helpful to me when you are as open as you have been today."

"Thanks, team," Michael says. "While we're on the subject of personal change, I told you at our planning meeting over the weekend that Brian was going to be available to provide executive coaching. As you know, I'm using Brian's services on a weekly basis for the next several months. Based on my experience with Brian, I believe he will be a key contributor to our change process."

"Michael, is it safe to assume that each of us can use Brian in the same way?" David asks.

"I would encourage each of you to call on Brian as an executive coach," Michael answers. "Have a good evening."

Your Turn: Be a *Change Agent*

1. What courageous conversations do you need to have with the members of your team who are underperforming? Have you looked in the mirror to assess how you've contributed to this underperformance? What more can you do to help members of your team succeed (e.g., provide clear expectations, immediate feedback, ongoing coaching)?

2. What are you doing to keep your high performers motivated? What more could you do? What could you do differently?

3. How effective are you as a role model when it comes to living the company's or organization's values on a daily basis? How often do you see others following your lead? What are your plans to deliver feedback to those who do not follow your lead when you model the values?

Doing nothing is doing something.

CHAPTER 9

▼

STAYING THE COURSE

"Our greatest glory consists not in never falling, but in rising every time we fall."
—Ralph Waldo Emerson

One Month Later

In the weeks that follow Roger's departure, Michael comes to realize it had been inevitable. He finds that Roger's leaving actually strengthens the bond of the executive team and their resolve to successfully execute their culture-change plan.

As part of their commitment to becoming role models for H&O's values, each executive solicits and receives ongoing coaching from Brian. The team moves ahead with renewed dedication. Michael's time with the Sales team provides him a fresh perspective on living the company's values. The challenges are exciting and fulfilling for him!

The next challenge facing the team is creating the annual budget for the coming fiscal year. Four weeks into the process, it is near the top of the agenda when they gather for their Monday morning meeting. Kim takes her place at the table and drops a large stack of papers, creating a "thud." She looks tired and seems tense. Michael makes a mental note of this as he greets the team. "Good morning. Did everyone have a nice weekend?"

"I wish you all could have been with me Saturday night," Alan says, smiling. "The symphony was in rare form. It was an amazing concert!"

"I heard about that. I'd have been there, but I was busy with my college reunion," Michael tells him. "It was wonderful to see some of my old buddies again."

"Incidentally, David," says Jen, "thanks for recommending that Thai restaurant to us. Ted and I loved it!" David nods and smiles.

"I'm glad you guys had fun," Kim snarls. "I was here working on the budget all weekend."

The room is suddenly quiet as it's clear to everyone that Kim is in a bad mood.

Michael says, "Well, we'd better get started." As is now customary at the beginning of meetings, he points to the poster of H&O's values (**I**ntegrity, **C**ustomer-Focused, **A**ccountability, **R**espect and **E**mployees First) on the wall and asks, "Does anyone have any 'I CARE' success stories?"

Jen and David describe positive changes they've observed in their areas. Kim is still silent. Next, Michael reviews the results from last week's Plus-Delta meeting evaluation and then turns the agenda over to Kim for an update on the budget process.

"As I said earlier," Kim begins, "my team and I worked all weekend trying to make sense of the input we've been receiving from the functional areas. As you can probably tell from my tone of voice, I'm not happy with the quality of what we've been receiving. The old adage 'garbage in, garbage out' applies here."

Alan begins to speak, but Kim cuts him off. She heaves a loud sigh and then continues. "Guys, as you know, I have to present next year's budget to the Board in six days. Although it's my responsibility, each of you is accountable for supporting the process by providing me and my team with accurate data. I don't feel this is happening—not by a long shot."

Alan tries again to answer. In a stern voice, Kim says, "Let me finish, Alan!"

Alan explodes. "Kim, I'm trying to help you with this! But if you'd rather just scold all of us, there's not much I can do for you!"

Kim's fatigue and frustration overwhelm her. "Go to hell, Alan!"

Michael intervenes. "That's enough! Everyone, please just stop and take a deep breath.

"Kim, I know you're tired. I also know that the budgeting process is not an easy one and that you and your team have been working hard on this. But making accusations and pointing the finger of blame will not help us make progress. I think it would be more helpful to come from a place of curiosity, as to why things aren't going the way they should be, instead of judgment. Brian told us issues like this would come up that would test us. Let's try to find our way through this together.

"Kim," Michael continues, "Do you feel we can move forward this morning in a constructive manner or would you like to come back to this after you've gotten some rest?"

Kim's tone is calmer, but she still seems frayed. "Michael, in all honesty, I don't know how I could possibly rest until the budget is presented to the Board."

"Kim," Jen says, "what I'm most interested in hearing is how my team and I can better partner with you and yours to make your life easier right now."

"Me, too," David offers. "How can I help?" Alan nods in agreement. "I'm sorry I snapped at you, Kim," he says. "I really am interested in helping."

"This is really nice to hear," Kim says, calming down a bit. "But you guys are killing me. I've made it as easy as I can for everyone to give me his or her numbers. I've distributed a template for each organization to use. But people aren't even using it. I can't get anywhere with this. My team and I are working with apples and oranges here."

Michael looks to the team. "Is this true?"

David answers first. "Kim, with all due respect, I think in your frustration you're exaggerating when you say that no one's using your forms. I couldn't figure out exactly what you were looking for, but I filled it out as best I could."

"We can do a post mortem later and sort out where the breakdown happened," Jen suggests. "How can we fix this now?"

Kim pulls out some of the budget spreadsheets and the team sets to work. She has highlighted the problem areas on each organization's template. One by one, they talk through the form to reach a common understanding and make plans to return the needed figures to Kim by close of business the following day.

"It sounds like we all have a lot to do," says Michael. "But before we leave the room, it's important that we talk about what just happened here and how to prevent it from happening again. This won't be the last time we're going to face a challenge or a crisis."

David glances up. He's sitting across from the values poster and sees the word "Accountability" facing him, as if in challenge.

"When I wasn't sure how to fill in your form, Kim," he says, "I should have taken the extra step to ask you about it and to make sure I understood what you needed from my team. That would have saved the costly re-work that we'll have to do now. And I apologize, Kim, because it surely would have saved you some frustration."

"Thanks, David," Kim says. "And I think I would have been better off bringing this up before we spent the entire weekend trying to sort through the mess. You know, I couldn't accept it when Brian said that *as your mood goes down, so does your IQ*. But I think I just proved him right."

Everyone laughs quietly.

"You know," she continues, "I thought I was making progress with this personal change stuff, too. I feel like I caved at the first real challenge!"

"Keep in mind," Jen says. "***It's all about progress, not perfection***. This kind of thing is going to happen as we continue on our culture-change journey. Sometimes it might feel like we take two steps forward and one step back. We've been working well as a team. Let's not be too hard on ourselves, particularly you, Kim. The good news is, we dealt with this accountably and respectfully—two of our key values!"

"Given the work we need to do in the next day and a half," Michael says. "I think it's time to adjourn our meeting. I think we just did our Plus-Delta. I want to thank everyone for the authentic conversation that took place here today. So let's get to work."

"Oh. One more thing before you leave," he adds. "I've got some good news. We have another round of interviews scheduled for the Sales executive position. As you know, our goal is to select two finalists from this group and have a new Sales leader in place in the next six to eight weeks. If any of you has time, I'd appreciate your participation in this round."

"I'm glad this has come up," Jen says. ***"I want to recommend that we carefully plan how we integrate this new executive into our team. If we want this new person to hit the ground running, we have to create an environment that will promote that."***

"Good idea, Jen!" Michael answers. "For now, I'd like you to work with Alan on that plan. Have a good day, everyone!"

Your Turn: Be a *Change Agent*

1. In highly stressful situations, how well do you hold to the leadership principles described in these chapters? In stressful situations, what is the impact of your behavior on relationships and results?

2. How effectively do you recover when undesired behaviors return? What steps do you take to identify and address the root cause(s) of undesired individual or team behaviors to prevent re-occurrences?

Continuous improvement comes from continuous learning.

CHAPTER 10

▼

REFLECTING ON THE JOURNEY

"Success is a journey, not a destination."
—Ben Sweetland

One Year Later

Having spent the past year working with his team to turn the company around, Michael now believes his legacy at H&O is secure. The work they have done is not only putting the company's finances back on track, but it is also creating a corporate culture that elicits discretionary effort. Now, he realizes, it's time to step aside as CEO.

He calls the team together on a Friday afternoon. Weekly Happy Hours were disbanded many months ago. Each of them is surprised to notice there is no agenda for the meeting. Their curiosity is aroused when Michael begins to reminisce about the past year. He retraces the steps they have taken in their journey:

- *Focus groups were conducted* with representation from all functions and levels within the company. Twenty desired behaviors have been identified that define Horton & Oliver's five values: Integrity, Customer-Focused, Accountability, Respect and Employees First.

- *Town Hall meetings were held* throughout the company as part of Horton & Oliver's new communication plan and were well attended. In each meeting, Michael was accompanied by one or more of the other executives and together they presented H&O's new vision and values.

- *Weekly customer meetings* provided Michael and other key Sales leaders the opportunity to share the future direction of H&O. More importantly, they listened to the customers' perspectives on how to improve service, quality, and pricing.

- *A new strategic plan was crafted,* incorporating the best internal and external thinking, and defining how H&O would differentiate itself and win market share from the competition.

- *Structural adjustments were made* within the organization to streamline customer focus and operating efficiency, and a new performance data reporting system was put in place.

- *Goals/desired results were refined.*

- *H&O implemented its culture-change education program* for management to:

  - Unfreeze old beliefs,

  - Shape new beliefs and behavioral habits aligned with H&O's values and associated behaviors,

  - Teach core leadership principles, such as accountability, to help shape H&O's new culture, and

  - Create a common language within the company and a shared reality among all employees regarding the direction of H&O and the values/behaviors necessary to succeed.

- *Each executive took his or her direct reports off site* for a two-day experiential learning session focused on the above. Those staff members, in turn, completed a learning session with their direct reports, until culture-change education cascaded through the management ranks of Horton & Oliver.

- *Every management employee attended a one-day workshop, "Values-Based Coaching for Improved Performance,"* designed to improve their feedback and coaching skills.

- *A revision to the Performance Management System now mandates formal bi-monthly feedback and coaching sessions for all employees.* Additionally:

  - The annual performance review and development process now incorporates H&O's values and associated behaviors, and

  - An online 360-degree feedback survey also has been incorporated into the performance review and development process so each management employee can receive feedback on how well they are living H&O's values, and so they can create personal development plans to make improvements.

- *Other HR Systems, including succession planning, compensation, hiring, and new employee orientation have been revised.*

  - In succession planning, the company commits to "promoting leaders who get desired results by exhibiting desired behaviors" (i.e., leaders who live the values of Horton & Oliver). This type of leader creates an environment where people volunteer their very best—in other words, they give discretionary effort.

- *The Waste-Not Challenge was implemented* across the entire company. A Six Sigma program for process improvement was launched to support this challenge.

The good news is that after months of hard work, the executive team's investment is paying off.

- Product quality and customer service have improved significantly.

- Customer satisfaction scores are up 12 points; market share is also up.

- A new culture audit of the entire company shows improvement in every area; although most items are still in the yellow or "caution" zone, no longer are there any items in the red or "danger" zone.

- Profitability and productivity are up and operating expenses are down, thanks to the successful implementation of the Waste-Not Challenge.

- Edward and the other Board members are pleased with the progress that has been made in a relatively short period of time.

After ten minutes of reflecting on the past year, Michael pauses. Having waited patiently for him to finish, Kim finally asks, "Is everything OK, Michael?" As he looks around the table, he realizes just about everyone on the team is looking at him with concern.

"As a matter of fact, Kim," he says, "everything is just fine." "There are so many positive things for us to celebrate—I'm so proud of what we have accomplished together. So, I hope it doesn't come as too big a surprise when I say that I have decided it's time for me to retire.

"Edward and the Board have asked me to stay until they complete their search for my replacement and I've agreed."

Team members step up to congratulate Michael individually. There are some tears. They thank Michael for helping to create a workplace they find personally and professionally rewarding. It is clear that, as sad as they are to hear he's leaving, they are grateful that Michael has been at the helm for their triumphant journey at Horton & Oliver.

Your Turn: Be a *Change Agent*

1. How will you know when you've been successful at shaping a new culture within your company or organization? What performance indicators will you use along the way to measure progress?

2. What are you prepared to do, from a leadership perspective, to re-shape the culture?

3. When you finish reading this book, what action(s) will you take? How can you become an even more effective change agent when it comes to improving your company or organization, your community, your life?

If it's to be, it's up to me!

EPILOGUE

▼

The achievements at Horton & Oliver were earned with commitment, hard work and careful attention to living the company's values. Under the executive team's leadership, H&O was on track to change the culture throughout the company within five years. They were fortunate. It typically takes a minimum of seven to ten years to inculcate culture change in large companies like H&O. Horton & Oliver was on the "fast track" because of these factors: a burning platform for change, unwavering commitment from the very top, Jen's expertise as a change agent, and guidance from Brian and his firm.

Members of the H&O executive team stumbled occasionally along the way, but they quickly regrouped by having authentic conversations with one another and by providing feedback and coaching. Regular coaching sessions with staff members and semi-annual executive retreats kept the momentum going. Today, focusing on both behaviors and results, having authentic conversations, and providing routine feedback and coaching remain integral to H&O's culture.

Success stories were shared each year at the Waste-Not Challenge Celebration. The Annual Family Picnic, once a way of life at H&O, was revived and became another occasion for sharing news of the achievements of teams throughout the company. There was one story that was first shared among the executive team. It involved a Sales manager who disliked a new H&O product line. Coached to approach changes with curiosity rather than judgment, the manager articulated his concerns to the Research and Development team directly. After an open discussion, in which each person acknowledged and respected each other's separate reality, and listened to one another's suggestions, the Sales manager became a champion for the new line. What's more, the design team gained valuable insights that benefited future product lines. The teams had begun sharing ideas as part of the culture-change process, but this conflict, which otherwise could have derailed those discussions, became an example from which both teams learned.

There were many more changes, as individuals throughout the company committed to living the values, not only in the office, but, also, in their personal lives. Kim continued to make gradual improvements, gaining confidence along the way. She soon married Bill and her H&O colleagues were among the circle of friends who helped the couple celebrate. At the reception, she thanked Brian for helping her strike a balance in her life. She took Jen aside and surprised her with a gift: a small mirror, in an elegant silver frame, on the back of which was inscribed: *"Thank you for helping me truly see myself. Love, Kim."*

Alan also seemed to gain confidence as things changed at Horton & Oliver. He assembled a team from various organizations within the company to develop his diversity initiative, itself an embodiment of H&O's values. The initiative was woven seamlessly into the HR plan. As the finances improved and positions were added, the company was prepared to welcome a diverse pool of candidates.

It was David who first started to track the long-term benefits of living H&O's values company-wide. Even before he began tracking his own coaching sessions, David had begun to study the lawsuits filed by departed employees and the value of consistent coaching in preparing a defense. He discovered that the process of coaching employees "up (to higher performance) or out" not only boosted morale, but it saved the company money. More employees began to acknowledge that they had been given ample opportunity to improve and were persuaded to drop their suits against the company. On a personal note, David negotiated an arrangement for himself that permitted him to reduce his work schedule at H&O, creating an opportunity for him to perform *pro bono* work for start-up companies.

Her first year as COO had been a busy one for Jen and she was proud of the part she had played in helping to turn H&O around. Still, she was surprised when Michael approached her to suggest she apply for his job. She and Ted talked it over between themselves and asked their children, Anna and Tony, for input before deciding to give it a shot. The Board appointed Jen CEO and the family celebrated with a vacation!

Before they left, Michael and his wife hosted a dinner party in the family's honor. The mood was light, as the team reminisced about their time together. Michael's wife beamed as she told them about the European trip the two were planning. "I guess 35 years is a little long to wait for a second honeymoon!" Michael laughed. "We'll just have to make up for lost time.

"I'd wish you luck," Michael told Jen, "but I don't think you or this team will need it!"

In the months and years that followed, Michael's name was mentioned time and time again as the leader who had saved Horton & Oliver and helped it become number one in the marketplace again. As part of his legacy, he became known as a change agent who had mastered the art of culture transformation!

About the Author

"Mark Sasscer has the unique ability to work with business leaders and help them transform themselves into change agents. He teaches executives that in order to change your company, you must first change yourself!"

—Jim Hinckley
CEO—Century Golf Partners/
Arnold Palmer Golf Management

"I've never before felt like a 'change agent' until working with Mark. His ability to help me rise above the mundane aspects of my job has taught me how to better focus myself and my investment teams on those activities that have a hugely positive impact on our success!"

—Chris Kleinert
President—Hunt Investment Corporation

Mark Sasscer is the founder and CEO of LeadQuest, LLC, an international leadership consulting and training firm specializing in leadership and team development, and organizational culture change. His clients include some of the largest and most successful corporations and institutions in the world.

Mark began his career at AT&T and spent fifteen years in the leadership ranks of the telecommunications industry. For the past twelve years, Mark has devoted his time and energy to helping senior executives of Fortune 500 Companies improve the way they lead. His personal mission is to improve the quality of organizational life by improving the quality of leadership. Through Mark's unique and motivating style of teaching and coaching, many executives have gained a deeper understanding of the impact that their behaviors have on relationships and organizational performance. Consequently, their companies have improved their business results.

Among his credentials, Mark holds a Master of Science Degree in Organization Development from American University in Washington, D.C, and a Bachelor's Degree from Towson University. He has earned several certificates in the field of total quality management and the science of applied behavior analysis. Mark has been a guest lecturer at the University of North Carolina, Loyola University, and Salisbury University on issues of leadership and organizational culture change.

Mark lives on the Eastern Shore of Maryland with his wife Cheryl, their three children, and their three dogs. You can contact Mark by e-mailing him at msasscer@leadquestllc.com. To learn more about Mark's company, you can visit LeadQuest's website at www.leadquestllc.com.